Ernie's Journey is a modern
woman) living in the fast-p
slows it down for us and be
purpose and meaning into i.
life is not worth living" Socrates argued at his trial centuries
ago. Mark Given and Don Greeson take a fresh look at that
age-old declaration and offer you some new ideas and tools
for your personal journey as you follow Ernie through his
satisfying quest for a more authentic life.

Jan Hodgson, Educator, Kansas City

*I had not quite completed the book when I was talking
with a person who has struggled for 5 years about a
personal issue. When he described his pain, one of the
stories in 'Ernie's Journey" popped into my head and I
shared it with my friend This grown man said: "I feel like
I could cry, you've just given me exactly what I needed to
get past this." I followed up with the fact that I couldn't
take credit for that wisdom, it was the book that I was
reading that gave me that profound insight. "Ernie's
Journey" can be life changing for you too.*

Coach Jackie Leavenworth, Cleveland

In *Ernie's Journey*, Mark Given and Don Greeson
have described the journey we all must take--
a journey to find your "Why!"

Zan Monroe, NC, Author of Stories of Uncle Adrian

FINDING MY WHY:
Ernie's Journey

A Tale for Seekers from
Mark Given *and* Don Greeson

Plan A ACHIE VEMENT

Mark Given
P. O. Box 1460
Roanoke Rapids, NC 27870
Cell Phone: 252-536-1169
markgiven@yahoo.com

Don Greeson
122 Rutledge Drive
Hendersonville, NC 28739
Cell Phone: 828-290-3627
dongreeson@bellsouth.~~com~~ net

Visit our Website at www.FindingMyWhy.com

First Edition: December, 2010

ISBN 978-0-615-40942-9

Illustrations by Olive Martini

Printed in the United States by Morris Publishing®
3212 East Highway 30
Kearney, NE 68847
1-800-650-7888

ii.

To our wives,
Janice Given and Jean Greeson,
the real muses

Contents

Acknowledgements

Though, as the disclaimer in motion pictures often submits, *any resemblance to real people or actual events is unintentional,* there are several people who have nonetheless contributed to this story from behind the scenes. They have made positive impacts, even if in seemingly small ways, and it is with genuine appreciation we acknowledge their contributions here. The first thanks go to our wives Janice Given and Jean Greeson, who know that the characters in the story sometimes actually do resemble our personalities, and not always in a good way. The other thanks are for the amazing investment of time and focus from close colleagues and fellow seekers who have generously shared their insights, corrected our grammar, and offered definition and clarity to those basic principles that create the platform for our tale (even if the ideas for it came from somewhere else in the universe.) These contributors include Jackie Leavenworth, Jennifer Dodge, Jan Hodgson, Anne Stokes, Danny Greeson, Evelyn Given, Elsie Jones, Zan Monroe, Corean Hamlin, and Donna Harnett. To all of them we are truly indebted.

Before you begin

Preface

The road leading to a goal does not separate you from the destination; it is essentially a part of it.   **Charles DeLint**

Ernie's Journey is not meant to be serious literature or the basis for a major field of study. But it may fill in some missing links in the evolution of personal achievement. It is about the quest for meaning in our workaday lives, not in the sense of experiencing some life-altering epiphany, but rather by examining routines and obligations to realize what may be better options. Why do we get up in the morning? What is *really* most important to us? Where is our passion? The answers can be simple or profound, painful or pleasurable, buried or in plain sight.

At one point in the story, our everyman hero Ernest Lee Goforth discovers he is able to clear a mental roadblock by examining a problem differently, or 'rephrasing the question.' Rather than concluding what the answer *is*, he finds it easier to conclude what it *is not*. In that spirit, it is easier to explain what this book *is not*, rather than define it in conventional terms.

- It *is not* a children's book (though it delivers its messages without profanity or what is often euphemistically deemed 'adult material.')
- It *is not* a prescription for success (though it may allow the reader to see his or her roadmap to achievement from a different perspective.)
- It *is not* a secret guide for revealing inner potential (though it may offer some common sense revelations for solving inner struggles.)
- It *is not* a spiritual or religious alternative (but it recognizes some benefits of spirituality unencumbered by dogma.)
- It *is not* a political narrative (but it does condemn the toxicity of polarizing political rhetoric.)
- It *is not* an original message (but it does incorporate some of the most widely accepted and potent principles offered by acclaimed philosophers.)
- It *is not* an academic discourse or psychological essay (but its comic structure supports serious themes.)
- It *is not* a true story (but it does offer parallels to real-life circumstances.

Who should not invest their time reading this book?
- People with no sense of humor
- People who believe they already have all the answers
- People who have made up their minds they cannot or will not change
- People who have already decided this book cannot or will not help them
    —*for whatever reason.*

Much of what happens in the story takes place inside Ernie's head, in the form of four different personalities he thinks of as his personal muses—the dude, the soldier, the werewolf, and the superhero. These aren't the classic muses of art and literature, but more like the "boys in the basement" Steven King describes in his book *On Writing.* Rather than the "airy fairy little female sprites that sprinkle happy dust," King's muses are blue collar guys who sit around drinking beer and telling dirty jokes, offering ideas when pressed and preferring not to be bothered. He makes it clear that these are the personalities he associates with the non-conscious mind. So it is also with Ernie, who is as much tormented by his muses as inspired by them.

This book also makes certain assumptions. It assumes, for example, that the reader has some basic skill set—training in a trade, recognized talents or special abilities, or a knack for working with people. It also assumes readers have a desire to succeed in ways that will not harm others and improve the world around them. If a reader's skills set and desire to succeed is not well defined, that's okay—neither were Ernie's.

Cereal Killer

Here we are, trapped in the amber of the moment.
There is no why.   **Kurt Vonnegut**

Y
ou might say the late night car wreck actually began that
afternoon, when a toddler eating Cheerios from her stroller tray
dropped a few of the little rings on the sidewalk. They remained there
despite interest from ants, beetles and birds throughout the day, and it
wasn't until traffic had all but disappeared—well after dark—that a
lone rat made the discovery. Scurrying across the street, his movement
caught the attention of a great horned owl perched nearby in a lofty
sycamore. Silently swooping down for the kill at the precise moment a
lone Camaro was picking up speed, the diving bird collided with the
windshield. The terrified driver reacted by involuntarily ducking and
jerking the steering wheel, causing the car to slam into a power pole.
The pole snapped, airbags deployed, and a street light went dark—all
within a second.

When Ernie—driving home from his job at the cinema—came
upon the scene, only two other cars were stopped shy of the
intersection. A huge yellow traffic light was still swinging at eye level
(Ernie didn't realize they were so big) from suspension wires that now
sagged between the broken pole and another one that appeared to be
leaning. It too was dark—in fact, the only light was coming from the
crumpled Camaro's headlights and the flashing strobes of a police car
aimed at it. Ernie watched as the officer walked toward the car with his
flashlight, glancing up and waving away others approaching on foot. It
was then that Ernie saw the bright flash and heard the pop, as a short
arc of lightning grounded a dangling power line through the flashlight-
wielding policeman.

The accident happened too late to make the morning
newspaper, but Ernie learned later from the TV's evening news that the
wreck's victim suffered only minor injuries. However, the policeman
died on the scene. He had a wife and a daughter. The driver, who
explained the collision with the owl, was not charged. In an interview
with reporters, a distressed police colleague volunteered that the
unfortunate incident was "a reminder that anyone could leave this earth
at any second."

It was true. Ernie replayed the scene in his head over and over.
At the multiplex he managed, he watched nearly every movie booked,
and it seemed as if almost all of them featured some form of trauma or

death. Yet to witness in person the accidental end of someone's life was infinitely more poignant. Whatever the recently deceased man had ever said or done was now history—there would be no second act, at least not in this life.

Thus, if you rewind events no further back than a mother's walk with her baby girl, you might accurately conclude that it was a few loose Cheerios that precipitated the fatal accident. By that logic, the same spilled cereal also began a personal quest to discover life's meaning for Ernie Goforth. You could also assume it was all a coincidence, but assumptions can be dangerous.

The Yellow Notebook

Six Sisters

> In the final analysis, the questions of why bad things happen to good people transmutes itself into some very different questions, no longer asking why something happened, but asking how we will respond, what we intend to do now that it happened. **Pierre Teilhard de Chardin**

"Over here! Over here! the muffled voice echoed from somewhere in the dense smoke and salty gulf-water froth. No longer able to feel anything and nearly blinded from the oily crude and blood coating his face, the exhausted petroleum engineer made one last desperate attempt to swim toward the voice. Light from the spectacular blaze of the exploding drill platform reflected off the roiling water in a moiré pattern, interrupted by the fishing boat's opaque shadow as the rescuing vessel came closer. The music reached a crescendo with crashing cymbals as a hand from the boat grasped the bobbing survivor's life vest and dragged him onto its bucking deck.

Sitting in the back row, Ernie thought to himself, "Man, they didn't waste any time making a movie about that!" *Safety Be Damned—in 3D* was already a box-office smash, and was showing on two of Ernie's multiplex screens. Well, only one of them was 3D, but both were sold out on Friday and Saturday nights. On the first wave of credits Ernie exited the auditorium, making his way to the door to be sure the soldiers of his uniformed army were at their posts. As he entered the hallway, the familiar smell of fresh popcorn seemed somehow comforting. Managing a theatre had its share of challenges, but protocol and procedures usually compensated for all but the most unexpected problems.

A new crop of customers for this latest blockbuster was forming lines at the concession counter, but there were no apparent issues to resolve and Ernie slipped into his office to call Glorianne. "The kids are all outside," she said with obvious pleasure. "Even Willy." Ernie knew what she meant by this, since Willy was usually in front of the TV playing video games. Sundays meant family time for most families with two young teens, but Ernie's "weekends" were

Mondays and Tuesdays. Thirteen-year-old William Ernest, or Will E.—and now just Willy—was somewhat awkward socially, a trait that Ernie saw in himself. His daughter Karma, on the other hand, was energetic and always inviting friends over—and even though she was not quite two years older than Willie, seemed to have nothing in common with him. There was a pause. "How are *you* doing?" Glorianne asked.

Ernie knew what she meant by this, too. He had been upset for the last two days over the Friday night accident. Witnessing the death of an innocent man just doing his job had really shaken him. No tragic music accompaniment; no rolling credits. No buildup, no warning—just a dark, quiet night punctuated by a flash and a pop. The story was finally on the front page of the Ordinary Observer, and Ernie had read it three times. "I'm OK," he said, "But I'm not sure the paper has told the whole story."

"I expect there'll be follow up," assured Glorianne. "What, with him leaving a widow and a child—you know the paper will have more on it."

Ernie realized she didn't understand exactly what he meant, but to be fair, even he wasn't sure what was missing from the news story. He told her he would see her around midnight. Any later and the projectionists' union would require overtime pay. Six Sisters Cinemas ran a tight organization.

The evening proved uneventful, except for the mouse, or some other scurrying rodent, in the parking lot. No doubt someone had dropped some popcorn. Two teenaged boys employed by the theatre chased it between cars with brooms, never finding their target, but drawing the attention of a shopping center security guard. Ernie calmly diffused the commotion that followed, thankful that he had known the suspicious guard since high school. (Ernie had played the saxophone; Big Ben had been a star linebacker. Neither of them ever expected to have night jobs at a shopping center when they grew up.)

Ernie was still thinking about the mouse and other wild creatures that come out at night when he finally made it to bed that night, which of course led his thoughts back to the owl incident. The episode repeated on his mental movie screen as he drifted off to sleep.

Nine o'clock on a Monday morning was early for Ernest Lee Goforth, but he thought that if he was early *enough*, he might catch the newspaper reporter at his office.

He was right—Al Wright was summoned by the *Observer* receptionist, and fresh from the week's first editorial meeting, seemed preoccupied when he arrived in the lobby. He wore jeans and a golf shirt, and despite summer temperatures, a sport coat that had seen better days. The receptionist indicated his visitor with a nod, and Ernie smiled and began, "My name is Ernie Goforth, and I live here in Ordinary. May I have a minute of your time?"

"Sure," the reporter said, hoping this might mean a scoop. "Let's go in here." Ernie was ushered into a small conference room with a round table and four chairs. The only window was one looking into the hallway just beyond the lobby. Wright closed the door. "Whatcha got for me?"

"Actually," Ernie started, "I wanted to ask you something about the policeman's death."

"The shock victim? Sad, huh?"

"Yes, very sad." Ernie studied the reporter's expression. "Your article said the car hit the power pole when the driver was startled by a big owl hitting the windshield, but there was no mention of why."

"Why what?" Wright asked.

"Why did the owl hit the windshield?"

Wright knotted his brow. "Are you serious? How would anyone know that? I suppose he was chasing something or just not paying attention."

"Well, you interviewed the police detective, the coroner, and you even talked to the driver. I was hoping you might have a theory." Ernie felt a little embarrassed. Maybe this was a dumb idea.

"Mr. Go—Goforth, isn't it? Even if I could interview an owl, this one was dead. My job is to report the facts as a journalist, not to speculate on an owl's motive or to offer my own theories. In my profession, we try to answer the questions of who, what, where, when, why, and how with straightforward reporting…"

"And you did that," assured Ernie, "except for the *why* question. It just seems to me that 'why' is—at least in this case—the most important question of all." Ernie immediately realized how idiotic this sounded, but it was too late to take it back.

The reporter sat quietly for a moment, staring at Ernie. "Why does ANYTHING happen?" he asked rhetorically. He threw up his hands. "Why do bad things happen to good people? Why do the stars keep on shining? Why do birds suddenly appear…" He smiled, almost sympathetically. "Look, I can tell this bothers you, but some questions are beyond the abilities of a reporter trying to make his deadline, and I'm afraid this question is one I'm not qualified to answer even without a deadline. Can you tell me *why* you feel the need to know? Or for that matter, even *why* you get up in the morning?"

Ernie felt uneasy. This whole conversation seemed a little silly. And, though the reporter was somewhat dismissive, Wright was right. Just like the facts in a newspaper story, Ernie knew when he got up in the morning, where, what and who he was, and even how he came to be a husband, a dad, and a theatre manager, but he couldn't answer *why* he was any of those things. He couldn't answer why he chose this lifestyle, why he worked in a job that tied up nights and weekends, or even why he got up in the morning.

"I see what you mean," Ernie said, offering a tone of humility. "I suppose very few of us understand the 'why' of almost anything. Maybe that's what people seek in religion."

"Well, I'm sure it's what they hope to find in religion, although I've discovered most churches preach to you 'why you should' rather than ask you 'what's your why?' In my humble opinion, finding what's right for you can't come out of a book or someone else's expectations. Everyone needs to find his or her own 'why,' the same way you would find your own 'what.' But hey—as a reporter, I seek answers for a living. If I believed I already had all the answers, I'd be a politician."

Ernie forced a laugh and thanked Wright for his time. On the way back home, he thought about the conversation, and not surprisingly those thoughts turned into one of his elaborate daydreams. His constant daydreaming was as much a curse as a blessing. All through school it had the effect of keeping him from concentrating, which translated into unremarkable grades, while simultaneously providing him a needed escape from unbearably boring classroom lectures, a process which (he believed) kept him sane. Now the daydreaming itself seemed a kind of insanity, an escape from embracing real-life quandaries head on. The 'why' question certainly qualified as a quandary.

He daydreamed about the journalist's list of five W's and one H, imagining them as the six sisters. In this mental cinematic scenario, jewel-bedecked *Who* was a status seeker, gift-bearing *What* was concerned with possessions, watch-carrying *When* was obsessed with schedules, suitcase-wielding *Where* was always traveling, and journal-posting *How* was dedicated to her writing career.

In his daydream, Ernie imagined them as antebellum damsels, with bustles and bonnets—characters who belonged in *Gone With the Wind.* Their movement and chatter was choreographed, each distracted in different ways with "the war" and their sacrificing father and their handsome brave boyfriends, and collectively concerned for their emotionally distant, hand-wringing sister *Why*, bless her heart. It was a quandary.

Almost home, his daydream movie was interrupted as he passed by the multiplex. He noticed the marquee's headline "Safety Be Damned—in 3D" and imagined in its place, "Discovering Miss Why—in Cinemascope." Then, passing the Walgreens, he remembered promising Glorianne he would pick up some shampoo, and turned into the shopping center. While there, a yellow spiral notebook caught his eye, and he bought that too.

The Dinner Party

> Flaming enthusiasm, backed up by horse sense and persistence, is the quality that most frequently makes for success. **Dale Carnegie**

When Ernie got home, Glorianne heard the door shut and called out, "Did you get the shampoo?"

"Yes, babe. I got your shampoo."

Glorianne came around the corner wiping her hands on a dish towel. "I'm making a special dessert to take with us tonight—Key lime pie."

"Take with us...where?" Ernie suspected it was a dangerous question, since Glorianne seemed to assume he already knew about this.

"To the Lumberknots, silly. Don't tell me you forgot we're having dinner with them tonight."

"On a Monday night?"

"Yes, Ernie. On a Monday night. Because one of their guests has to work most other nights. Now who do you think that person is?"

"Okay, okay—I totally forgot we were invited to Ashe and Cherry's for dinner. Who else did you say was coming?"

"Well there was going to be one other couple, but Cherry said that an older, retired couple had just moved in across the street and she wanted to include them as a welcome to the neighborhood.   So now it will be us, their friends Robert and Steven, and their new neighbors, the Fences, or the Fenceposts, or something like that."

"Are the kids coming?"

"Our kids? No—they were invited but neither expressed any interest."

For the rest of that Monday, Ernie did routine household chores. While mowing the yard, he thought about a distraught Miss Why and imagined her looking into the distance, asking the universe what her purpose in life might be. Why was she born? Why did *she* get up in the morning? And then, in the dreamscape, he heard orchestra music and the ethereal voice of Gerald O'Hara. "You mean to tell me, Katie Scarlett O'Hara, that Tara doesn't mean anything to you? That *land* is the only thing that matters. It's the only thing that lasts." And as she pledged to return home because 'tomorrow is another day' even Scarlett realized her *why*.

The mower's engine began to skip, and then came to a stop— as did the lush strings of *Tara's Theme* playing in Ernie's head. He discovered the gas tank was dry. He looked around at his own piece of land—a suburban lot of about 1/3 acre in a treeless subdivision named 'The Woods.' Perhaps *land* was not the reason he got up in the morning.

That evening, Glorianne and Ernie arrived at the Lumberknots at 6:40, appropriately ten minutes after the appointed time, and almost simultaneously with Robert and Stephen, whom they knew from other social gatherings. (In fact, everyone seemed to know Robert and Stephen.) The Goforths waited for Steven to park the Prius at the end of the driveway before jockeying their green VW Beetle beside it. The Beetle was supposed to be Glorianne's car, but somehow she wound up with the family SUV and Ernie always drove the Beetle to work. Glorianne had put up her golden hair to show off her most dangly earrings, and wore a long, satiny red dress with a matching shawl. As she stood by the car—one hand on the open door—to put on her high heels, Robert approached her and said without inhibition, "Oh, Glori honey, I just LOVE your dress! You look fabulous!" As Ernie fumbled with not one but two Key lime pies, he momentarily looked at his wife standing on one leg and realized she did indeed look fabulous.

Ashe Lumberknot introduced the Goforths to his new neighbors Colonel Vince Pickett and his demure wife Trula, who had just moved to Ordinary from Fort Bombastic. The retired Colonel stood erect and projected a steely demeanor, allowing a much shorter Trula to exchange most of the pleasantries. His tanned complexion contrasted with his buttoned-up white golf shirt, which seemed to be a deliberate match to his short white hair. Trula, on the other hand, was festively plump, and wore a bright blue dress with yellow butterflies fluttering all over it. Her hair was perhaps a little too red to be natural, and to Ernie she looked like a child's drawing of a woman. Though soft spoken, she expressed herself with grand arm gestures and exaggerated facial expressions; her enthusiasm serving as counterpart to the Colonel's stoic presence.

The Lumberknots had no children, but compensated by being somewhat childlike themselves. No doubt this dinner party would have some sort of theme, or they would play some game. Ernie hoped he would survive the evening without a reason to feel embarrassed. Having the animated Robert and Stephen there was a good thing, he thought, because they loved parties and Ernie could probably sit quietly in the background. Time would tell.

Glorianne joined Cherry in the kitchen, while the men and Trula sat in a large room with floor-to-ceiling windows filled with treasures from the Lumberknots' many trips to exotic places. Behind the sofa was a carved screen, with the face of some Hindu god surrounded by an intricate pattern, and a trio of African masks with contorted faces painted in unnatural colors. Potted banana trees and assorted tropical house plants formed a miniature jungle along the windowed walls.

"Oh, I absolutely LOVE this room," announced Robert, who wore a shirt that seemed to match the foliage. "This is my idea of heaven!" Ashe handed him a glass of clear liquid with ice and green leaves swirling in it, and Robert placed his right hand on his heart while accepting the glass with his left.

The Colonel studied a framed photo of a picturesque village. Boxy white houses with red-tiled roofs were clustered on a hill cascading to the sea. He turned to Ashe. "Greece?"

"The Isle of Capri. One of my favorite spots on earth."

The conversation danced around the room, engaging everyone except Ernie, who felt left out. Apparently, everyone but him had traveled extensively. He had only journeyed to other countries through the movies. Those trips had dramatic beginnings and endings, with each adventure lasting approximately two hours. And everywhere he went the exotic food tasted like popcorn.

At dinner, the guests were all seated in assigned chairs. Several courses were served, with a quasi-theme of Gulf coast cuisine. Ernie thought about *Safety Be Damned—in 3D* and the environmental nightmare portrayed in the movie, and considered the shellfish he was consuming a reminder that the place, and the tragedy, were real. It was all interconnected, he thought—the world, the people and animals in the world, and the seemingly small actions that had ripple effects on everyone. But he was daydreaming again.

"Okay, I want everyone to look under his or her plate, and there you'll find a slip of paper," announced Ashe.

Oh, no, thought Ernie. A party game. He was terrible at party games.

"Before we have the lovely dessert Glorianne brought, I thought we would have a lively discussion. I've primed the pump with a different question for everyone. Robert, I'd like you to read your question out loud."

Robert sat back in his chair and ceremoniously opened the folded slip of paper. He read slowly, enunciating every word as if on a Broadway stage. As a lawyer, no doubt he'd had practice in the courtroom. "If you could assume the identity of any celebrity, who would it be?" Closing his eyes and folding his hands on his lap, he sat quietly for a few seconds, and Trula squeaked a giggle. Without opening his eyes, he said theatrically, "Oprah Winfrey."

Laughter and clapping hands rewarded the answer. Stephen rolled his eyes and told the group, "He thinks he is already."

"Why would you want to be Oprah?" prodded Cherry.

"Because she is a born uniter. Think about it—while politicians and those awful blowhards on radio and TV divide the country into this group and that group and work to alienate people, Oprah is busy bringing people together. Honey, I'd love it if I had the power to bring people together—to give everyone something they can all agree on."

Trula leaned forward and clasped her hands. "You are so right! I think Oprah has a purpose on this earth, and the country is blessed to have someone like her."

The Colonel was smiling politely but said nothing. Ernie was studying him when Ashe suddenly said, "Ernie, tell us what your question asks."

The table grew quiet as Ernie unfolded his slip and read, to his horror, "Why did you choose to work at a theatre?" His first thought was, 'Oh, so that's why the chairs were assigned!' Though he was certain the Lumberknots had no idea how profound the question would seem to him, he was still stunned that they would actually choose a question for him that involved the word 'why.' In a split second, Ernie decided to refrain from offering any depth to his answer, and instead to pretend this subject was of absolutely no concern to him. He took a breath, shrugged his shoulders, and said, "I love popcorn!"

Again, everyone laughed, and Ernie was safe. No one challenged the answer, and the next question went to Glorianne—something about "if you could choose to be any animal…" and so on. It all seemed trite as they took turns around the table until the Colonel was asked to read his question.

Sitting perfectly erect, the old soldier purposefully unfolded the paper and read, "What determines success?" Everyone was quiet and sat motionless while the Colonel composed his thoughts. No one was sure how the new neighbor might answer. Ernie was expecting some simple phrase like the ones he had read on motivational posters, or maybe a quote from Gandhi about becoming the change you want to see in the world. But if nothing else, Col. Pickett was methodical, and surprised his fellow guests with a short lecture for a successful military campaign. It was delivered with an air of authority.

"Employ the four A's," he advised. "Attitude, Affirmation, Awareness, and Action. These are key elements for any successful endeavor once you understand how they work together. Attitude is simply knowing—knowing without doubt—that your mission can and must be accomplished. Affirmation is determining the steps necessary to complete that mission, and planting them deep inside your mind. You do that by writing them down and repeating them often. Awareness is being alert to both opportunity and deterrent, the idea being that your environment can serve as an attraction to—or a detraction from—your goals. And finally, Action is the execution of the plan. To answer this question, Success is determined *in advance*—as soon as you commit to employing all four A's."

"Bravo!" Robert exclaimed with genuine appreciation. Others around the table seemed impressed as well. Trula smiled proudly. Ernie decided this was something he needed to remember: *The Four A's*. His imagination began creating ways to remember all of them. Maybe they could be the four aces in a deck of cards…

"Everyone ready for pie?" Cherry announced more than asked. "Let's take it in the lanai."

Guests began to migrate toward the sunroom with its travel trophies. Ernie decided the Lumberknots were excellent hosts—the questions on hidden slips of paper were brilliant. Funny how he had been asked why and the Colonel had been asked what. Less funny is how the Colonel's answer was complete and his was, well—not complete.

That night, Glorianne got ready for bed and did not question her husband's need to stay up awhile. Anything before midnight was, after all, early for Ernie. When the house was quiet, Ernie retrieved the yellow notebook he had purchased that morning. On the first page he wrote, *Finding My Why.*

On the next page he jotted down, *Six Sisters; Who, What, Where, When, Why, and How.*

On the third page he wrote, *Four A's: Attidude*—

Ernie's daydreaming started again. He had accidentally written Atti-*dude*. Well, he mused to himself, that would be a great way to remember Attitude. Atti*dude* could be this cheerleader guy with long hair, always saying things like, "We can do it, man!" and cheering on the mission. Then he wrote A-formation for Affirmation, imagining Col. Pickett demanding a written plan. The new spelling seemed appropriate, a formation of a plan to be memorized by affirming it repeatedly. A character with that name might actually look like the Colonel.

This was working! Attidude, Aformation, and now... Awareness. Or, A-*were*ness, spelled with w-e-r-e as in the word werewolf. Maybe. Too much of a reach?

For a moment, Ernie struggled with the negative image. Well, a werewolf is a mythological 'changeling,' alert to his own nature, and aware that something could trigger a major shift in his form. A*were*ness could be the guy who is always on the edge of becoming a wolf so therefore has to be alert at all times—to his circumstances, to his surroundings, and to his intentions. Okay, it's corny, but Awereness it is.

To Ernie's ears, the final A—Action, even sounded like a Superhero, so he added Actionman to the list of personified A's. The characters represented, for him, a clever way to remember the roles each A-word would play in a future mission. He decided to call his A-list of personalities "The A-Team" after the famous TV show of his youth and its revival in a 2010 movie. He also decided that he should show no one his notes— they might decide he was a danger to himself and others. He chuckled quietly at the thought. Though he often referred to himself as just plain ol' Ernie, deep down he knew he was not like anyone else in Ordinary.

Meeting the Muses

> No one can give you better advice than yourself. **Marcus Tullius Cicero**

That same night, Ernie decided to scribble what he could remember about the various roles of the four A's, or his imagined "A-Team." For amusement, he began to picture what each team-member might actually look and sound like. As he gave voice to Attidude, he made him sound a little like Jeff Bridges in *The Big Labowski.* "You know, man—like, really cool."

Aformation was no-nonsense and had the authoritative tone of Col. Pickett. When Ernie began to imagine hearing his voice, it was in the form of a question. Aformation was asking him, "Ernie, at the Lumberknots, why did you affirm that you were terrible at party games?"

'Wait a minute! Just by giving my imaginary friend a voice doesn't give him permission to question me. Or does it?' Ernie wondered.

"Call me a muse if you want," the voice of Colonel Pickett sounded in Ernie's head. "The fact is, you affirmed your belief that you are terrible at party games and sure enough, when it was your turn to answer a question, you just made a joke of it. You chose to not participate. In other words, you determined your failure before you even began the game."

Ernie stared at the words he had written in the yellow notebook. There was not even a drawing of Aformation, and yet the imagined character was already coaching him.

"Your vision of me is stronger than that of the others because you have a clear image in your mind of what I look like and how I sound—thanks to the inspiration Col. Pickett provided. Once you begin paying attention to the others, their images will also become clearer, and you will understand that they are all integral parts of you and your abilities."

What kind of drugs had been in his food tonight? Ernie had always possessed a vivid imagination, but he'd always had control over characters of his own invention. This one was trying to control *him!*

"Promise me that in the future, you'll not decide you are bad at something before you try it. Promise me in the form of an affirmation. Okay, soldier?" Aformation meant business.

Ernie could see his military "muse" more and more clearly. He wore aviator-style sunglasses and camouflage fatigues. He stood erect and carried a clipboard. He was looking directly at Ernie, waiting for an answer. Ernie said, "Okay," and realized it was out loud. Aformation handed him the clipboard which now held the notebook and told him to write it down. Ernie wrote *I will not decide in advance that I am bad at something.*

Aformation took the clipboard from his hand, turned it around, and examined it. "The wording is a bit awkward, but we know what you mean, don't we son?"

"Yes, we do." Again, Ernie spoke out loud to the voice only he could hear…and to the character only he could see.

"Far out, man! That is so weird! He's like, not even really there but you can totally see him!" Attidude's voice was quickly becoming more defined. "You know, man, you could see me too if you just believe you can. I, for one, absolutely know you can do it."

Ernie stared into a dark corner of the room, and the Dude began to take shape. Some cheerleader! He was wearing dirty tennis shoes, wrinkled baggy pants, and a sloppy sweatshirt with a big collegiate letter A on it. The A was yellow. His straw-colored hair was in dreadlocks, and he had one of those awful chin beards just under his lower lip. Despite the purposely disheveled look, Attidude carried an old-fashioned cardboard megaphone. Ernie hoped this strange figment was not actually a part of his personality, but it worried him that because the thought of it had come so quickly, it might be true. "Well, man? Can you see me?"

"Yep," said Ernie out loud. "I can see you. You are not exactly what I expected."

"Yes, he is" corrected Aformation. "You get what you expect to get. Your image of Attidude is a direct manifestation of your somewhat sloppy beliefs in your own ability. *He* knows you can do whatever you believe you can do, but *you* don't quite believe in him yet. When you start seeing Attidude as a reliable, valued component of your mission, he will appear differently to you. Do I make myself clear?"

"Yes, sir!" Ernie said to his powerful imagination.

"Man, that was like, awkward. Your own creation was dishing it out to you – about ME! Wow! I kinda like what he said though, don't you? Maybe it's time we all met the others on the team. What was that other dude's name? You know, the 'werewolf' guy?" Attidude had put the megaphone between his knees and drew "air quotes" when he said werewolf.

Ernie said, "Awereness." And no sooner did he say the word—or in this case, the name—than a dark, brooding hairy guy with rounded shoulders appeared in the corner of his eye. The figure frowned slightly, squinted, and looked left and right, occasionally doing a double-take at some perceived threat. He did not look straight at Ernie.

Attidude said, "Yep, you've spotted him. I can see him too, man. He looks a little scary, don't you think?"

Aformation weighed in. "He's as scary or as harmless as you picture him. Awereness' role is to stay alert to both danger and opportunity. At the moment, he's a little apprehensive about all this because you are. When you decide he's a valued part of your team, his appearance will change. But be forewarned: You don't want to do anything to trigger his rage, or he will live up to his reputation."

"You mean, he'll turn into a wolf." Ernie blurted.

Awereness, suddenly realizing the conversation was about him, crystallized into a vivid image and answered in a coarse whisper. "We're all werewolves. The whole literary genre of the man/wolf thing is based on the realization that we still have wildness in our souls. You're lucky. Unlike most men, you have another layer of protection from your internalized beast—me."

Ernie pondered the implications. In a nutshell, because he had Awereness on his team, he could be alert to the threat of primitive responses present in everyone and could better control his own impulses. Ernie remembered how the Colonel had said, "Your environment can serve as an attraction to—or detraction from—your goals." It seemed natural that others might revert to animal instincts—fear of change, for example—to distract or deter someone from personal achievement. The trick might be, then, to simply eliminate from your environment those distractions that create obstacles in your path to success.

"Oh, it's not that simple. There will still be plenty of obstacles in your path," Awereness cautioned. Ernie forgot that Awereness could read his mind—or rather, was part of his mind. It slowly dawned on him that there was nowhere to hide from his own thoughts, as long as his internal check and balance system was characterized, literally, by individually manifested concepts. The A-Team was now part of him.

Who or what sparked the next thought, Ernie was unsure, but suddenly a superman figure wearing blue tights and a red cape, billowing despite any detectable breeze, landed directly in front of him and placed his yellow-gloved fists on his hips. A large, sparkling emblem in the basic shape of the letter A emblazoned his muscular chest—again, in yellow. There could be little doubt this was Actionman. Ernie thought he saw some resemblance to himself, as if looking in a funhouse mirror that made him look more buff. It occurred to him that perhaps the others mirrored his image, too, and he glanced at the trio standing in the background. Sure enough, Awereness was a coarser, more rugged and barefoot version of Ernie in jeans and a plaid shirt, Aformation was a lean, tanned version of Ernie with a crew cut and shades, and Attidude was his lazy, sloppy opposite. Ernie recognized them as different parts of his own personality.

Awereness whispered something to Attidude, who came alive and began cheering, "He's HERE! He's HERE!" through his megaphone, as he jumped up and down. The out-of-shape cheerleader then started coughing from the exertion.

Actionman jutted his jaw and thrust his chest as if displaying his signature 'A.' "I am Actionman. You must be Ernie." Ernie was surprised by his own creativity. His imaginary character had just taken the initiative to introduce himself, as if it came from someone else's mind entirely. Actionman was polite, but made no acknowledgement of the other team members. He was supremely confident, but seemed to be waiting for Ernie to make the next gesture or comment. Unlike the others who came into consciousness with advice and admonitions, Actionman was silent, but decidedly statuesque.

Awereness approached Ernie and whispered a raspy message into his ear. "You have to tell him what to do. Once he knows your instructions, he will fly into action. Thus the name."

Actionman stood at attention, his satiny cape still unexplainably blowing like a flag in the still air. Ernie admired this superhero version of himself, and was relieved that he didn't talk much. "Nice to meet you, Actionman." Actionman smiled and nodded, ever so slightly.

Ernie stepped back and looked at the entire A-Team. 'What a bizarre creation,' he thought. If the team shared that thought, they ignored him. And then Ernie asked, "So how do I summon you? Do I simply think of your names, or do I have to say something out loud?"

"We're always behind you, soldier, watching your back," Aformation answered.

"Totally! Woo Hoo!" Attidude enthusiastically added.

Aformation continued in the Colonel's memorable voice. "By the time you realize you need to summon one of us, we'll already be engaged. *But*, how good we are at our jobs depends entirely on your trust and belief in our ability. To enhance that belief, you will need to write down your goals on my clipboard, and repeat them daily."

"And you'll need to listen to my scouting reports," Awereness added, sounding more and more like Al Pacino. "It's important to know what's happening all around you."

"You give me the word, Boss, and I'm all over it" *Actionman* assured him, and he thumped his chest once with both fists—partly to punctuate the commitment, partly to salute Ernie.

Then Ernie heard a voice coming from the cardboard megaphone, "This is AWESOME!"

"I made you some coffee, Ernie," Glorianne was saying from some other dimension. Ernie's mind was drifting like that exhausted petroleum engineer—the one bobbing in the water who could barely hear someone calling from the fog. "I'll put it here on the table beside you."

Ernie opened his eyes to a sunlit room. "Have the kids already left for school?" Glorianne either ignored him or didn't hear him. She had wandered off into the kitchen.

"You never came to bed last night, Babe," she said from the other room. "And you were talking up a storm in your sleep! Talk, talk, talk. I decided I would never get any sleep if I made you come to bed so I just let you sleep in the chair." She emerged from the kitchen with a plate of food, fork and napkin.

"Have the kids already left for school?" Ernie repeated.

"Yes, Ernie. Over an hour ago." She set the plate down beside the coffee and took a seat on the sofa across from the recliner. "What did you have to drink last night when I was in the kitchen with Cherry?"

It took Ernie a moment to realize this was an accusation. "I don't know. Ashe was mixing some drink called a Mojito, but I only had one. It was okay, I guess. Why?"

Glorianne sighed dramatically. "It must have been potent, that's all I can say. Well, that's all I'll say about that, anyway."

Ernie reached for the plate that held a muffin and some fruit, and noticed his yellow notebook also lying on the table. Placing the plate on his lap, Ernie began peeling off the muffin's crusty overhang with his fingers. "So, what else?"

As he pushed the crust into his mouth, he looked up at Glorianne, and saw his support team—all four A's—sitting around her, watching and listening. Awereness was gesturing, putting his hand first behind his ear and then pointing to Glorianne, as if to say "listen closely."

"Well, there's something important I need to ask you."

Cosmic Encounters

<u>*Spectator*</u>

> Life is not a spectator sport. If you're going to spend your whole life in the grandstand just watching what goes on, in my opinion you're wasting your life. **Jackie Robinson**

Ernie sat nervously on the chair, partly because he felt anxious about Glori's important question, and partly because he really, really had to go to the bathroom. "Honey, I don't want to interrupt — *honestly* — but I need to hit the head for a minute. I promise I'll be right back."

He left Glorianne sitting there looking down at the carpet and hustled down the hall. Still dressed in last night's clothes, he caught a glimpse of his image in the mirror. Shadows from whiskers competed with shadows below his eyes for the "least attractive" superlative. After answering Nature's call, he studied the mirror again and noticed for the first time two unfamiliar spots on his complexion.

"Do you see the REAL Ernie in there?" quizzed someone with a coarse whisper. Still observing his image, Ernie's eyes shifted to see the reflection of Awereness standing behind him.

"I see someone who looks remarkably like my father," admitted Ernie.

"Time is moving on, Ernest," the werewolf said.

"Where's Attidude when you need him?" Ernie joked.

"Hey, man, it's early," whined Attidude, sitting on the edge of the tub. "But I need to wake up, because I'm feeling a vibe. Whatever your lady wants to talk about, you'd better be agreeable."

"You told the Mrs. you'd be right back," reminded Aformation.

"Yeah, I'm going. This bathroom's a little crowded anyway."

When Ernie re-entered the living room, Glorianne had poured herself another cup of coffee and sat on the edge of the sofa. Her expression was serious, but not threatening. "Ernie," she started, "remember we were planning a vacation in the next few weeks when school lets out?"

"Yeah...?"

"Well, last night at the Lumberknots, Cherry was telling me about this week-long retreat she was taking with some of her old college friends, and it sounded very exciting."

"What does that have to do with us going on vacation?"

"Well, it seems that one of the gals has a conflict and there's an opening. They all signed up for this workshop/retreat weeks ago and all the plans are set. Except they've got reservations for four and only three can go. They're one person short." Excitement was creeping into Glorianne's voice.

Ernie was still waiting for his wife to ask a question, but she now seemed to be waiting for him to respond. 'Why is she telling me this?' he thought, perhaps a little too clearly. Ernie felt a slap across the back of his head and flinched. He raised his hand in response, but realizing it was one of the A-Team who hit him, transferred the reaction to simply smoothing his hair.

"Oh, I see!" Ernie finally answered. "Cherry asked if you wanted to go along with them, right?" He saw her smile and take a sip of coffee, her eyes bright and eager, and added, "I think that's a great idea!"

"You DO?" Glorianne nearly spilled her coffee as she sat upright. "But I'm afraid it will interfere with our vacation plans. I was hoping maybe you can reschedule your time off and we can go some other week."

Attidude turned his megaphone around and pointed the small end at Ernie's ear. He then spoke softly into the bell end. "Like, that was the easy part, man. Now is when you have to stay positive!"

"You know, you have always adjusted your schedule to fit mine—I'm sure we can figure this out. What kind of retreat is it?" As Glorianne launched into an excited explanation of the *Cosmic Encounters* week, the mouthpiece whispered, "Excellent job, man!"

Ernie sat and listened intently, decorating his muffin with strawberries and banana before washing it down with coffee. By the time Glorianne was describing the Trust Exercises, Ernie's imagination began to compete with her voice. He wondered what strawberry popcorn might taste like. Or maybe banana. Still looking at her as she spoke, he noticed her lips moving but heard nothing but a distant babbling that finished with the words 'Costa Rica.'

"Costa Rica! This seminar is in Costa Rica?" The megaphone, apparently still beside his head, said, "Chill, man. It's okay! It's okay! This could be a good thing!"

"It's a retreat, Ernie. A woman's retreat in the jungle. Haven't you been listening?"

"I'm sorry Glori—I missed that part. Wow, that IS exciting! What an opportunity! Don't worry about the kids and me. We'll do fine."

"Oh, I'm not worried. Willy wants to go to computer camp with Lester that same week, and Karma has been invited to the beach with some girls from the drill team. Oh, Honey, this will be so great—and you can have time to read those books about movies you've been collecting."

Well, it was true that Ernie had a pile of unread books with titles like *The Golden Age of Cinema* and *The Real Wizard of Oz*. But it bothered him that his entire family had made plans that excluded him. Even if the kids would rather join their friends than spend a week with their parents—no surprise—Glori and he *could* spend that same time together. But she was genuinely excited about this trip, and on the advice of Attidude, Ernie concealed his disappointment.

Attidude reassured him. "I'm telling you man, this could be a good thing!"

Glorianne wasted no time getting on the phone to Cherry, and while Ernie got ready for another day, he thought again about the suggestion of a week alone with his library of books on cinema. He enjoyed movies—and he considered managing a theatre a good fit for him—but every time he read a biography of Jimmy Stewart or a history of Metro-Goldwyn-Mayer, he felt a greater sense of distance from that world than being closer to it. The truth was, Ernie had little to do with movies—his role at the theatre was counting box office receipts and checking employees' time sheets. He was responsible for changing the marquee and cleaning the bathrooms. And though the books' photos and narratives of Alfred Hitchcock movies provided glimpses of the movie-making craft, they also underscored Ernie's awareness that he was an outsider to the industry. If he were honest with himself, he dreaded a full week of being reminded that movies—or even his surface involvement with movies—was not his 'why.' It was an interest, but not a passion.

"So, do something about it." There was a dry, raspy tone to the whisper. Ernie looked up to see Awereness in the bedroom mirror.

"If you're a werewolf, how is it I can see your reflection?" Ernie challenged him.

"You must be thinking about vampires. Don't mix your myths."

"Okay…so what do you mean, do something about it?" Ernie noticed the other A-Team members waiting for the answer as well.

"How long have you been escaping from real life? One day you live in ancient Rome, cheering on a gladiator; the next you're in South Africa watching a soccer match. Yes, there are victories to be celebrated and great truths to be realized, but in the meantime you aren't contributing anything yourself. Ernie Goforth, you're a spectator—not a participant."

"Oh, dude! That was like, cold!"

"Well, he's right, actually." Ernie was now looking directly into the mirror. "Maybe it's time I tried to do something about it."

Awereness caught his hesitation. "What is it Yoda said in *Star Wars*? 'Do or do not. There is no try'? You must decide—and once you decide…"

Aformation finished the sentence in the voice of Col. Pickett. "Success is determined *in advance*—as soon as you commit to employing all four A's.

Actionman, always listening in silence, suddenly broke his stance and grabbed the clipboard from the stoic soldier. In a blur, he was placing it in Ernie's hand, a pen dangling from a string attached to it. Aformation said, "You know what to do."

"Yeah—well, sort of. What exactly am I writing down?"

Aformation answered, "How about simply, 'I will no longer be a spectator, but a participant. I will find my true passion and act on it.' It's a little awkward but we know what we mean, right?"

"Oooh, that's awesome!" said Attidude.

Ernie was not sure it was awesome. "Okay, I'm writing it down but I still don't know where or how to begin."

Awereness whispered, "You have already begun by writing it down."

"Well said," confirmed Aformation.

Ernie knew Glori's suggestion of postponing the family vacation would not fly. For all the meticulous scheduling he did at work, he was a poor organizer for his own family. There would be no way he could reschedule a trip—Six Sisters Cinemas had a policy that required the district supervisor or a new hire to stand in for a manager taking time off during the busy summer season, and regional SSC managers had already scheduled vacations. The next opening was in the fall, after school started. His vacation time would be spent solo. Ernie decided to keep this information, at least for the moment, to himself.

For the next several days, Ernie watched over the operations of the multiplex, placed ads in the paper for upcoming attractions, and recorded new automated phone messages. He replaced movie posters, updated the theatre website, and placed orders to replenish concession inventory. Knowing how much of the company's profit margin depended on sales of candy and popcorn, he watched the habits of customers—so many of them treating the snacks as an integral part of their movie experience. He noticed, too, the patterns of most theatre patrons and thought that not much had changed since the days of Bonnie and Clyde. He had some ideas for the company about traffic flow and display, and seeing Aformation standing there by the velvet ropes with his clipboard, dutifully wrote them down in the yellow notebook. If given the opportunity, he would someday share some of these ideas with senior management. "You know we could visit headquarters while the Mrs. goes to Costa Rica," Awereness whispered. "We could impress them with your insights."

"We really could do that, man! Let's totally do that," the Dude added.

"Maybe," Ernie answered with the tone that he was not sure this would happen. Attidude glanced at Aformation, who was shaking his head in disappointment. Awereness looked grimmer than ever. Ernie thought he might have even heard a low growl.

Gentle Thunder

Fit no stereotypes. Don't chase the latest management fads. The situation dictates which approach best accomplishes the team's mission. **Colin Powell**

Days of indecision turned into nearly a week as the retreat, computer camp, and beach getaway grew nearer, Ernie felt no closer to knowing how he might act on his commitment to finding his true passion. The idea of visiting Destiny City where Six Sisters was headquartered had merit, but he wasn't sure his ideas warranted such a long trip. He was, he realized, very much an observer, a 'spectator,' and could not see himself as a consultant to senior management. Actionman stood by constantly—fists on hips and cape billowing—but Ernie provided him little to do.

Every day grew a little longer, the sun a little hotter. Willy wasted them in the den playing video games, often with Lester, except when his mother insisted he turn off the machine. She couldn't complain about his grades. He would easily pass the sixth grade, and was in fact near the top of his class. But it was Karma who enjoyed the outdoors, and it was Karma who enjoyed an active social life. Glorianne was comforted in knowing that the conscientious parents of Karma's best friend Whitney would be beach trip chaperones, and assured Ernie—who barely communicated with his kids—of her safety. A full week before the retreat, Glorianne started preparing oversized meals so there would be leftovers for Ernie to eat in her absence. This way, she surmised, he would not fill up on popcorn.

Then, on the last Friday night before school let out for the summer, Ernie was in the lobby of Six Sisters and heard trouble outside. There was the unmistakable thunder of heavy motorcycles, several of them in fact, cruising through the parking lot. He looked outside to see how, one by one, they parked diagonally in an area to one side of the building, and watched as each leathered, booted rider dismounted. Ernie counted eight altogether, and as engines grew quiet and they gathered on foot—some began to take off their helmets— Ernie noticed that several, no wait—ALL of them—were women. Patrons watched suspiciously as the gang stepped into the glare of the lighted entrance, helmets in hand, and it was then that Ernie realized they were not only women, but senior women. 'The Granny Gang?' he mused to himself.

Anticipating their destination, Ernie stepped inside the ticket booth so he could get a closer look through the window. One short, Rubenesque woman with unnaturally red hair came forward and asked in a soft voice if they could get a group discount in addition to senior citizen discounts. She looked familiar.

"Trula? Excuse me—aren't you Trula Pickett?"

"Why, yes dear. Oh, you're the man who loves popcorn! What a nice surprise!" And Trula's eyes lit up. "This is your theatre?"

"Yes ma'am." Ernie then whispered in the teller's ear. The young man objected quietly, "But we don't honor discounts or passes on Friday nights…" and Ernie assured him he would initial each one.

"Oprah recommends *Safety Be Damned* so we decided the whole club should see it together," Trula explained as they stepped inside. "Ladies, this is Ernie Goforth. He runs this beautiful theatre." The mature women smiled sweetly, and after some ticket thank-you's and lobby compliments, one asked if they might use the lounge.

"Oh, of course!" Ernie replied and gestured down the corridor. "You'll need to show the girl at the ropes your tickets."

Trula continued visiting while the others left, rearranging chains and scarves as some headed toward the velvet ropes and others toward the concession counter. For the first time Ernie noticed the pink lettering on the backs of their black leather jackets, which read, 'Iron Butterflies' and in italics below that, *Fort Bombastic*. Ernie was at a loss for words, the A-Team nowhere in sight. Finally he said, "Is the Colonel a motorcycle enthusiast?"

"My land, NO!" Trula replied. "Vince is afraid of the things. But he supports our cause, which is to bring a little fun into people's lives. Not only ours, mind you—but others who sit around on their fat *be*-hinds fretting about getting older. It's never too late to make a contribution, even if it's nothing more than to challenge stereotypes."

Ernie wondered if she was referring to the public's impression that motorcycle gangs are comprised of sweaty men with arrested maturity. Or did she mean that no one expected little old ladies to ride Harleys? It didn't matter. Whichever it was, she was right.

"Oh, we do other things than just ride around, mind you. But when we volunteer as a group, we always ride together to draw attention to our cause. It's just like the Red Hat Society, except that we ride Fat Boys."

"Exactly like it," Ernie agreed as Trula fished for the ticket she had dropped into her helmet. "Tell me, what inspired you to join a motorcycle club?"

"I suppose I got the idea after attending the most wonderful woman's retreat—something called Cosmic Encounters. Do you ride?"

"No, my transportation is a green Beetle."

Trula smiled and gave Ernie a look that said, 'that's too bad.' "Well, I must go—don't want to be late for the 'Damned' movie!"

Ernie was simultaneously amused, concerned, and inspired. 'The old gal must be in her late 70s,' he thought. He made a mental vow that he, too would be an inspiration to others when he reached her age.

"Write it down," said Aformation. "But don't limit yourself to being an inspiration after you retire. Write down that you will impact other people's lives from this day forward." The camouflaged soldier was holding out his clipboard. Ernie asked "How am I going to do that?" and realizing he was asking out loud among the patrons, gestured for Aformation to join him in his office.

Safely inside, Ernie asked again. "How could I possibly make a daily impact on others?"

Awereness appeared in the room to answer, "You'll know How when you discover Why."

Still doubting, Ernie opened the yellow notebook and glanced up at Aformation's authoritative expression before writing—just past the passage that read *I will no longer be a spectator, but a participant*—a new affirmation. It said *I will endeavor to positively impact the lives of others every day, even if in seemingly small ways.*

Aformation turned the clipboard around to read it, and commented, "Excellently worded, friend. You're getting better at this."

"Thank you." Ernie then took it back, and as if to show the A-Team he could make his own decisions, added yet another passage: *I will journey to the Six Sisters Cinemas headquarters in Destiny City and consult with Senior Management about my ideas for enhanced revenue—and about an enhanced role with the company.*

Aformation read the new entry and showed the clipboard to the other A-Team members, all of them now assembled. Ernie saw each of them applauding. Awereness howled in appreciation.

Attidude joined in the canine song. "Woo Hoo! Good for you, dude! That's like the only way you're gonna get noticed, man!" He made an attempt at some leg kicks and then, breathing hard, plopped onto a folding chair.

As his smile faded, Awereness asked Ernie, "And why have you decided to do this?"

Ernie was not sure. "Maybe it's time I took some initiative and actually did something to further my career," he speculated.

Awereness stared at him, his expression grim. "Yes, but WHY? Is that your passion—to further your career? Or is it to make more money? Or do you really mean to have more control over your workaday existence? Maybe you mean you want to have more time with your kids?"

"Well, that's the whole point now, isn't it? I don't exactly know why. But at least I'll be doing something productive, and maybe I can figure it out." Ernie was perturbed, and for a moment considered firing his team. But that would mean giving up—the lazy way out.

The other A-Team members were watching Ernie's exchange with the wolf man with great concern. Attidude decided Ernie would not be receptive to a pep talk right now, and Aformation understood that Ernie had not reached a recordable conclusion. Actionman seemed distant, and for a moment, his cape fell flat. As if to add insult to injury, Awereness taunted him with his raspy tone, "Trula seems to have it figured out."

Attidude looked at the others with an impish expression. "Is he going to join the Iron Butterflies?"

Ernie decided to focus on business and re-entered the theatre to begin the process of auditing ticket sales and counting receivables while the last shows were playing. The ticket squad began their housekeeping assignments. At 11:15, auditorium doors were opened to facilitate the exiting crowd. Ernie waited to speak to Trula and the Butterflies.

"So, are the club members heading their separate ways now? Or do you have plans for a midnight ride to terrorize the town?"

Mrs. Pickett smiled, waved her arms, and said with a hint of mischief, "Actually, we're headed over to my place to terrorize the Colonel! And then tomorrow morning we'll have breakfast at Bob Evans and ride over to The Forks to visit the monk."

Ernie's eyebrows arched. "The monk?"

Iron Butterflies began to flutter around Trula. One of them—as tall as Trula was short—waded into the conversation. "Don't tell me you don't know about the monk! Around Ft. Bombastic he's a legend."

Ernie answered with a question. "So, you're not talking about some biker bar named *The Monk*, but an actual monk?"

Trula spoke up. "I suppose he may not be a real monk, and no one is sure. But there's no doubt he's a very wise man, and he lives alone in a converted grain silo over in The Forks. A lot of people visit him to get his advice on matters. If you've never met the monk, you should go!"

Several Butterflies were zipping jackets and putting on gloves and Ernie realized they needed to leave. He cut the conversation short. "Maybe I will! You say he lives in The Forks—over in Wayward County?"

Trula repeated. "In a grain silo. You can't miss it—it's just beyond the old railroad trestle."

"Okay, then! How was the movie, ladies?"

Several voices answered at once. "I'll never buy from that oil company again!" was heard with "I never realized their stockholders still got dividends—it's ridiculous!" and tangled up with "Tomorrow I'm gonna ask the monk what he thinks!"

The next day, Saturday, Ernie woke to the sounds of cars crashing and for a moment thought there was an accident on the street. Then he realized it was the TV and, of course, the sound was from one of Willy's video games. As he stumbled down the hall and into the kitchen he noticed both Glori and Karma were sorting their wardrobes. Their departure time for adventure was nearing, and the Goforth women were steadfast in their preparation.

Willy, like Ernie, was putting things off as usual. The last day of school was Tuesday, and travel for everyone began the following weekend. Ernie's last day before the scheduled vacation was Sunday, so he would see everyone off before leaving for Destiny City. He realized it was actually a little late to be confirming his company substitute and making an appointment to see the VP of Development, but he would do that first thing Monday.

"Monday?" Aformation asked. "Why not right now? You don't work on Monday—what makes you think everyone else does?"

Ernie vowed to call and at least leave voicemail messages for his colleagues as soon as he brushed his teeth. Or maybe he could send an email.

Suddenly Actionman landed in front of him. "We'll follow up with an email," he said. "But first we'll call."

Ernie brushed his teeth with Actionman standing beside him watching and waiting, fists on hips. With minty-fresh breath, Ernie checked the SSC website for the numbers and made the calls. To his surprise he actually reached his district manager, who assured him he was covered and safe to leave for vacation on schedule. Ernie then left voice and email messages for the Development VP—a man named Morris Better. Aformation made him make a note that he would follow up again on Monday.

"Good job!" Attidude said, and Ernie noticed that his cheerleading muse seemed a little more awake and cheery than usual.

Ernie then asked Glorianne to join him for a cup of coffee on the screened porch. "I'd love to, Ernest Lee! How sweet!" He then told her about his plan to visit Destiny City to share some operational ideas and talk to the big guys about potential advancement. Glori was encouraging. He then told her about Trula Pickett and the Iron Butterflies, and before the cups were washed, Glorianne was on the phone to Cherry Lumberknot.

"Did you know Trula Pickett rides in a biker gang!?"

The Monk

There are things known and there are things unknown, and in between are the doors of perception.
Aldous Huxley

Early that afternoon, Ernie checked in at the theatre and asked his assistant to watch over the matinee shows, and reminded her that he was as close as his cell phone. "Next Saturday will be busy, but you should be fine today." He had an errand to run.

The community known as The Forks got its name from a series of streams that came together to make the Wayward River and formed a lush, fertile delta ideal for farming. With the big military base nearby, some of the pasture and crop land had given way to sprawling builder developments—the kind offering your choice of three basic floor plans in four architectural styles. But The Forks still had remnants of the family farms that once dominated Wayward County, and after an hour's drive, Ernest spotted the lone silo standing like a sentinel over the stream just beyond a railroad trestle from another era. Ernie slowed his green Beetle down to determine which dirt drive lead to the white cylinder and spotted a mailbox with the name AHA.

His tires created a growing dust cloud despite the attempt to drive slowly toward the unusual residence. A chicken ran across his path, and Ernie could see a couple of one-story wooden structures— low barns, really—in the trees beyond the cinder-block silo. There was no car and no evidence of anyone home as he rolled to a stop just a few feet from the door, a storm door, no less, that looked odd shielding the entrance of a grain silo. Above it was neatly painted, "Tower of Power."

As Ernie opened his car door, he saw more chickens parading. As he visually followed their path, he noticed a flabby pig puddled in a wallow, his head raised to observe the intruder. They were studying each other when Ernie heard a slow, sing-song voice say, "Welcome, my friend. I am Aha."

Aha was bald, barefoot, and dressed in a bleached white robe tied with a plaited rope sash. His face was cherubic—his cheeks, pink—and he was bowing slightly with his hands folded together at his waist, fingers laced. 'You have to be kidding me,' Ernie thought. Aha did indeed look like a monk,

"You have questions," Aha stated. "I would like to hear them. Please come in."

Somewhat skeptical, Ernie looked for his A-Team. When he spotted them, they were all smiling—even Aformation—like children who had just been invited in for ice cream. The Dude had two thumbs up.

Ernie followed Aha into the tower, where there was a small wooden table and two chairs below a low ceiling. The only light came from the transparent storm door, but Ernie noticed a well used, unlit candle on the table. A set of narrow wooden stairs followed the curved wall up to a dark opening in the ceiling. "Would you mind following me upstairs?" Aha asked. "You are a practical man."

"Oh, that's fine!" Ernie said, secretly happy that he would see more of the converted silo. He was unsure what Aha meant by "practical man," but it didn't bother him. Ernie imagined that a featherbed cot, some old scrolls or perhaps some ancient wall tapestries would greet him upstairs.

But upstairs—beyond the hole in the ceiling—Ernie realized there was another door—this one solid—and when Aha swung it open, there came with it a blast of cold air. Aha's tower was air conditioned! Inside, a large window opposite the entrance (and hidden from the road) allowed the sun to pour in and Ernie was shocked to see a flat screen TV tuned to ESPN. Aha caught his surprised expression and said, "I too, am a practical man." He picked up a remote control and turned off the set.

Aha explained that his office, computer, and counseling room were on the top floor, and above the silo was his satellite dish. "Cell phone reception is great," he added in his sing-song voice.

"So how did you get the name Aha?" Ernie wanted to know.

"That's your question?" Aha teased. "Actually, A.H.A. are my initials. My full name is Allison Harrison Anderson—which always sounded to me like names for 'My Three Sons.' I really don't like the names Al and Harry, so I just called myself Aha.

"So what's with the robe?"

"Wow, Ernie, you really have profound questions! The robe is just a comfortable…"

"Wait a minute—how did you know my name?" Ernie was both surprised and suspicious.

"Oh, the Butterfly ladies were here this morning and said you'd probably be by. Trula said she thought you drove a green VW, but I didn't expect you so soon." Aha's kind smile and pink round face suddenly looked more street savvy than spiritual. "And you do have questions."

"Yes, I do. But my first question is 'are you really a monk?'"

"I'm a counselor and personal coach. But I find peace in this rural landscape and here I feel no obligation to dress up. Besides, I've discovered that some clients respond better if they think of me as their spiritual guide. The first session is always free, and allows people a chance to see if my advice will work for them."

"So you're not really a monk."

Aha smiled benevolently and answered in his sing-song style. "I suppose that depends on your perceptions. Does it matter? Do you think that wisdom only comes from cloistered study or pure intent? Will my advice be somehow more valuable if you believe I practice monastic rituals? In the end, you will accept what fits into your own paradigm of beliefs, so the most I can offer you is to help you focus your personal energy."

Ernie heard a raspy voice whisper into his ear. "This guy seems pretty sharp. Let's hear what he has to say, regardless of how he lives or dresses."

Ernie let down his guard. "What exactly do you mean by personal energy?"

Aha chuckled. "Okay, let's start with that and then you can share with me the reason for your visit." Aha gazed out the window into the clouds. He spoke slowly, his voice rising and falling for emphasis. "Whether you are a student of science or a student of spirituality, the great lesson you will ultimately learn is that everything is interconnected. We are surrounded by and comprised of energy, which some consider cosmic forces and others as molecular movement. It doesn't matter—everyone agrees that energy is literally everywhere and makes up everything. Your body is an amazing chemical factory, converting the energy stored in food and water into a vessel of consciousness, able to transmit and receive energy. The sum of your experience and your gifts channels that energy and enables you to influence your surroundings—even your future."

Ernie interrupted. "You lost me. I understand that energy is part of everything, but..."

Aha stopped him. "No! Energy is not part of everything—it IS everything, and the portion you possess is your personal energy—to do with as you choose. Remember what they taught you in seventh grade? Matter cannot be created or destroyed, only changed? It's true, and energy is what changes it. A tomato seed converts sunlight, water, and basic elements from the soil into a plant, which produces a tomato, which provides your body with nutrients and the energy to grow and function, and one of those functions is thinking. Thought can create still more ways to convert energy.

Look around you—everything in this room, from your T-shirt to my television, began as a *thought*. Just like the tomato plant that converted basic elements using energy, the man who ate the tomato converted the nutrients into energy that nourished thoughts that ultimately resulted in a T-shirt and a TV."

Ernie thought this sounded ridiculous. "It sounds like you're trying to tell me that sunlight and dirt produced a TV. That's silly! It was the focused effort of developing an idea and years of experimentation that produced the TV. The only energy *that* required was brain power."

Aha smiled. "Exactly! Brain power is energy!"

Ernie felt challenged. He had driven all the way to The Forks to ask a monk for guidance—or at least for some perspective—and now he was discussing some pedestrian version of quantum physics with a strange man who may or may not be a monk. But he had to admit that Aha had a unique way of looking at things. And the A-Team seemed fascinated.

"Okay, but what about the ideas themselves? Does the tomato convert the water and sunlight into, well, ideas?"

Aha answered, "You mean consciousness streaming?" He then studied Ernie to decide how to explain. After a pause he began, "Have you ever heard someone say, 'It suddenly occurred to me...' or 'The idea came to me...'?"

"Sure. But those are just expressions."

"Really? Do you think people who use those expressions actually believe their ideas are their own invention? Or is it more likely, they simply realized something that was already a fact? Imagine ideas as waves of thought passing through space, sort of like radio waves in search of a receiver, bouncing around for anyone to intercept them. If a problem or question exists, a solution or answer also exists. You just have to *find* it."

Ernie saw Awereness nodding. Aformation tapped on his clipboard with the pen. Ernie confessed, "I guess I never really thought of ideas that way—that they're just out there for the taking."

Aha continued, "Well, it's not like going shopping. I mean, you have to ask the right questions to get the right answers. Sometimes your non-conscious already knows the answers but your conscious mind hasn't quite assimilated them; sometimes you have to open your mind to receive the answers from beyond the physical world. People have different ways of understanding this—through contemplation, meditation, or prayer. So ask the questions you had for me, and maybe I can suggest a way to find your answers."

Though he had rehearsed this moment in his mind, Ernie struggled to find the words to express his one big question. He started by admitting that, though he loved the cinema, he was tired of working nights and weekends. He loved his wife and children, yet often felt disconnected from them. He earned enough money to get by, but not enough to feel secure or afford nice things. He had an overactive imagination, but lacked a creative outlet. In short, he felt dissatisfied with his life and had no sense of purpose. If he could just find his passion, an answer to *why* he was here, he would then know what to do with himself. Ernie concluded with "My only question is, how do I find my *why*?"

"Wow," Aha said. "That's pretty insightful. Okay, this is my chance to live up to my reputation. Can you tell me what triggered all this? In other words, when was your 'Aha!' moment?"

"I think it was the night, about a month ago, when I witnessed the accidental death of an innocent man trying to help others. In the process of asking why he died, I found myself asking why I'm alive."

Aha's response was unexpected. "That's not an Aha! moment, that's an Oh No! moment. Don't confuse the two. You may be on the right path,   but I think it would be wise to stop associating the question 'why am I alive' with 'why did he die.' You should focus more on what inspires you and less on what frightens you."

Aha looked up, then down, as if pondering a problem. "You are a practical man.   My advice is to practice being positive.   Use that imagination of yours and think about how you might change the world for the better. Be aware of the opportunities around you. Connect the dots. Listen to the universe. Once you recognize possibilities, create an action plan, and channel your personal energy into the project. There's little doubt in my mind that you'll begin to understand your *why* in the process. Besides, you've practically told me why already." Aha bowed slightly and clasped his hands. It was a subtle dismissal.

Ernie was hoping for a magic bullet. Instead, he got a bunch of BBs. Connect the dots? Listen to the universe? Channel your personal energy? Despite Aha's enigmatic answers, Ernie was pleased that he had visited 'the monk' and had someone to talk to. Aha was a bit of a mystery himself, but he seemed genuine and Ernie had no problem thanking him before descending the curved stairs.

Exiting the Tower of Power, Ernie again saw the lazy pig peering from his private wallow, and turned to wave good-bye to Aha. "What's the pig's name?"

"Happy!" sung Aha. "Use the circle drive to turn around. Good luck!"

Ernie cranked the engine and aimed his car for the loop around the Tower of Power. When it passed by the little wooden barns, Awereness whispered, "There's his car." Ernie could see through an opening the grill of a shiny white BMW.

"You've got some things to write down," said Aformation.

Routine

The Phone Call

> As long as habit and routine dictate the pattern of living, new dimensions of the soul will emerge.
>
> **Henry Van Dyke**

A s the green Beetle cruised back to Ordinary, Ernie's cell phone began playing the funk classic, "Tell Me Something Good" and he glanced in the mirror to see where he was in traffic before answering. The phone I.D. read "Ashe L."

"Hello Mr. Lumberknot!" Ernie said on speaker.

"Greetings, Goforth," the tinny speaker voice answered. "Cherry tells me that Glorianne is going with her to Costa Rica and that your kids are abandoning their old man the same week. I just called to ask if you wanted to join me in some mischief while everyone is out of town."

"Wow, what a great idea. Actually I'm headed out, too. But what did you have in mind?"

"Oh, I don't know. Something out of your normal routine. Maybe go to a movie—"

"Ha. Ha. You know me so well."

"So where are you going? Aren't you working next week?"

Ernie suddenly realized how his answer would sound. He was using his vacation time to visit his employer's headquarters. He decided to make it sound like a business trip, which it kinda was. "I'm going on a road trip," he answered, "over to Destiny City."

"Destiny City? Pray tell, why in the world would you choose Destiny City?"

"That's where the company headquarters is," he explained, "and I'm going in for meetings on how to improve concession sales."

"Seems a bit unusual to have strategy sessions just as the summer season begins! Whose idea was that!?"

Ernie's first thought was not how to answer Ashe's question, but rather how remarkable it was that his friend was so intuitive about his business. Well, any business. Ashe Lumberknot was one of those people who seemed to always be ahead of the game whether it was selling a company's stock ahead of a market dive, or buying a distressed property ahead of a big box store's need for it. Ashe seemed to have perfect capitalist timing—and here he was again, instantly aware of a planning flaw. Ernie had to come clean.

"Actually, it's my idea. I see some opportunities for enhanced revenue through new packaging, traffic flow, coupons..."

"Good for you, Ernie!" said the tinny speaker voice. "How are you presenting the numbers?"

Ernie sat silent for a moment. The numbers? He realized he didn't have anything to actually show management—just the ideas to discuss. "Well, it's not a formal presentation. It's more of a suggestion that the theatre might benefit from re-thinking the status quo."

This time it was the speaker that fell silent for a moment. Finally Ashe asked, "Well, you have actually tried these techniques at your own theatre, right? Surely you have some receipts or inventory analysis you might share to support how this could work for the whole chain..."

Ernie was horrified. Ashe was right, of course. And now the idea that he might actually impress his superiors seemed silly. If anything, they would be DE-pressed that a moron like Ernie Goforth ran one of their multiplexes. Still driving—but now truly distracted— Ernie saw a convenience store parking lot ahead and decided to get off the road. He answered Ashe as the car slowed down to turn. "Well, no," Ernie admitted. "I just have some ideas and I thought it would be better to discuss them before I implemented them behind their back."

"You're a good soldier, Ernie," came the response. Ernie waited for Ashe to continue, but the speaker was silent.

"There's a 'but' coming," Ernie challenged.

"Well, I'm sure you have some good ideas, but—okay, yes, I suppose there is a 'but'—I think the only way you're going to accomplish your goal is just—well, DO it. My bet is that if you simply go suggest some ideas, they'll be forgotten by the end of the day, or they'll assign them to someone to study and that will be the end of it. People are so married to their routines that it takes something dramatic to shift their direction or to change their thinking."

Ernie now was sitting in a parking place with the car engine turned off. His focus was on the conversation. "How would *you* do it?"

Ashe laughed. "Me? In a word, I wouldn't. No offense, Ernie—it's just not how I think. I'm the guy that would package the idea in some way and SELL it to the chain. And I would sell it by showing your management how much money they're losing by not using my services, rather than how to enhance what they're already doing now. But hey, that's just me. Call it a character flaw."

Ernie thought of the Lumberknots' beautiful home and the photos of their world-wide travels. He remembered that many of those trips were taken as business trips—pursuing some idea for a new distribution method or a new import service. Ashe represented the epitome of Aha's advice to "connect the dots."

"You know, you're right. Maybe I should slow down and rethink this thing."

"You mean postpone the trip? So you're up for getting together while the ladies are away?"

"I'll let you know. I need to think this through."

"Okay, my friend. I realize it's short notice. Give me a call when you've figured it out!"

"You got it. And thanks for the invite." Ernie pressed the 'end' button on his phone and sat staring at the highway. He heard the voice of Col. Pickett.

"Don't you dare."

"Dare what?"

"Don't you dare postpone this trip. Your friend may make some good points, but if you don't go to Destiny City you'll just fall back into your old routine."

Ernie thought, 'There's that word again.'

Aformation continued, "Plan the work; work the plan. You've made a commitment, you've written it down, and you must follow through."

Ernie protested, "Yes but what if the plan is flawed—what if you realize it's not thought out, and you should abandon it before making a fool of yourself?"

The soldier was ready for him. "So, adjust your strategy. Change your tactics. Don't abandon the mission altogether! The A-Team will be with you every step of the way."

Just then Awereness whispered, "Now might be a good time to write down the monk's advice, before you forget. I especially like the thing about being aware of opportunities around you."

Ernie picked up his yellow notebook and scribbled, *Be aware of opportunities. Connect the dots. Listen to the universe.* He wondered if Ashe Lumberknot qualified as a representative of the universe. There was something else—oh, yeah—*Channel my personal energy.* He then looked at his watch, cranked up the Beetle and got back on the road.

The Dream

> One travels to run away from routine, that dreadful routine that kills all imagination and all our capacity for enthusiasm. **Ella Maillart**

That night, after work, Ernie quietly slipped into bed and kissed Gloria good night. He tried to push the A-Team out of his mind, and did his best to think of anything but the trip. But, true to the "Law of Attraction," the more he tried to avoid imagining the trip, the more his mind traveled along its path. Finally, perhaps from sheer fatigue, he drifted into a deep sleep. Unfortunately, his non-conscious mind continued the journey in the form of a vivid dream.

The green VW was entering a nameless town. Ernie was looking for the directional signs to Destiny City, when he spotted a sign for 'Normalton.' In his dream, Ernie had always heard nice things about Normalton—how it was a simple and pleasant community. Perhaps he should at least take a look around to see what Normalton had to offer.

"No!" he said aloud, imagining Aformation's authority. You've made a commitment, you've written it down, and you must follow through.

"No, what?" said a voice that sounded as if it came from a cell phone speaker. Ernie looked out of the car window toward the electronic voice and spotted a slender man who had been crossing the street. The pedestrian came to a stop at the command, his head turned toward the car window.

"Oh, I'm sorry, Ernie responded. "I didn't mean you…"

The slender man turned his head almost mechanically forward and continued walking across the street. His gate was stiff, and Ernie thought he heard some sort of whirring noise as his legs moved methodically onward through the intersection. He watched him continue toward a diner, its parking lot full of cars. Just then a horn sounded and Ernie realized the light had turned green and he was holding up traffic.

"What in the world is going on?" he asked himself. Ernie glanced over his shoulder one last time before turning on his signal to exit the street. In the dream, it was lunchtime, and he might as well have lunch at the diner where the mechanical man was going. Maybe he could find out who or what he was.

The diner's sign said, 'Aunt B's Home Cooking,' but its overall appearance reminded Ernie of all the marginal places with wholesome, friendly names that served predictable, bland food. The abundance of cars in the parking lot attested to its local appeal. He found a place along the side, locked his car and entered the establishment, which offered varnished wooden booths with rolls of paper towels and trays of condiments. The booths had the same simple structure as the monk's wooden table. To his surprise, the mechanical man was sitting alone, just two booths in. "Hi, welcome to Aunt B's" was heard above the din, and Ernie realized the greeting was meant for him.

"Hi," Ernie said to the dark-headed hostess. "Before I'm seated, I need to speak with that man for a moment," He gestured toward the second booth.

"Oh, you mean Routine? Sure—he's here every day. I save him the same table." The young woman whose name tag said Heather was matter-of-fact, and volunteered a plastic-covered menu. "Wanna sit with him?" Before Ernie could answer, Heather called out, "Hey Routine! Want some company?"

"Sure, I'd love to meet a new friend," came an electronically amplified response. Ernie saw his mouth move, but the lips did not seem to sync with the words. He smiled and sat down on the uncomfortable wooden seat across from the strange man. Heather left two menus, though she already knew what Routine would order.

"In case you are wondering," the mechanical man said, "my name is Routine. I am a robot." Despite the oh-so-obvious clues, Ernie was not prepared for such directness. Does he mean he's really a machine? Ernie weighed his next question carefully.

"My name is Ernest, and it's good to meet you. I'm afraid I am not at all familiar with robots. Would you describe yourself as part man, part machine?"

"I'm afraid I am not part man, part machine" responded Routine. "I am all machine. But I consider myself a practical machine." The electronic words were pleasing in their delivery, but Ernie couldn't help but notice a lack of expression in his eyes. They were, after all, artificial eyes in a dream setting.

"I confess I am fascinated that you are a machine but you function as if you are human! I mean, you are even in a restaurant." Ernie realized he was enunciating his words as if speaking into a voice recognition system, which of course he was.

"I confess I am at this restaurant because the food has plenty of oil in it, and I require a balance of fibrous material and oil to function properly."

Makes sense, Ernie thought. Routine was indeed practical. He studied the robot for a moment. The skin looked real enough, and he was wearing a blue collared shirt and khaki pants. Except for an oversized monogram, the outfit was just like what anyone might wear. "What do the letters WIT on your shirt mean?"

Routine explained, "The letters WIT on my shirt mean Wave Induction Technology. It is the method by which I learn to think and converse."

Ernie was fascinated. "You actually learn to think? How does that work?"

Routine sat quietly for just a moment longer than one might expect, as if formulating an answer. At least that's how Ernie interpreted the pause. Then, rather than responding with the already annoying habit of rephrasing the question, Routine explained his extraordinary ability by withdrawing a message from deep inside his data banks.

"I learn to think by intercepting and replicating the energy field from brain waves created by the humans around me. In case you are wondering, my maker realized that as with all electrical wiring, even circuitry in the brain emits faint magnetic fields, which can be captured with very sensitive receptors. Once received, the signals can induce patterns which may be converted into what some people call artificial intelligence. But I think you will agree that there is nothing artificial about me."

Ernie then saw something he had not noticed before. With a click, Routine drew his artificial lips into a smile. Of course, his eyes did not move, and the smile was that of the now iconic "hideous clown" of which horror movies are based. Ernie drew back in response and felt a chill.

Suddenly Heather appeared. "Y'all haven't been waited on yet? Tell me what you want to drink and I'll get things started. Course, I know what Routine wants. He always gets the same thing, don't you Routine?" Still smiling, Routine pivoted his head toward Heather and the smile disappeared—his expression mercifully returned to a simple stare.

"I will have my favorite beverage, thank you," said the robot politely.

"Uh, I'll have a Pepsi," said Ernie.

At almost exactly the moment Heather left, a petite blond girl named Tiffany appeared and asked, "What can I get you to drink?" When Ernie explained they had just ordered, Tiffany twisted her mouth into the same smile Routine had, except her lips did not click. She simply said, "Well then, I'll be back in a minute to take your order."

Ernie looked at Routine, forgetting for a moment he was a robot, and blurted, "I wonder why she didn't just ask us what we wanted to eat?"

"In case you are wondering," Routine said, "the ordering process does not work that way. First you are seated and given menus, then you order your beverage, then you order your food after your beverage arrives. This is how it is always done."

"Is this something you have learned from reading minds—to believe things are always done the same way?"

"This is not something I have learned from reading minds. It is the way I am programmed. Once I have learned from others how something works and integrated the method, there is no need to examine it for alternative methods."

Ernie was not sure he quite grasped this logic. The robot seemed to be saying that once a way of thinking had been established, there was no reason to find new ways of thinking. It occurred to Ernie that this could be a bad thing if the behavior or attitude originally learned was misguided. Once ingrained, a habit was hard to change.

Tiffany arrived to deliver the Pepsi-Cola and a coffee cup filled with what looked and smelled like cooking grease. Ernie was afraid to ask. She then took their orders—or actually, just Ernie's order. He told her he only wanted a grilled chicken sandwich and some fries. Tiffany assured him it would be coming right up.

"I always order the same thing," Routine said in his speaker voice. "Corn. Aunt B's Home Cooking serves excellent corn."

Ernie decided to ask the mechanical man about his programming. "So, Routine, if your program is designed to integrate the thoughts of others, are you ever concerned that you may be picking up bad habits?"

Routine said, "So, Ernest, you are concerned that once I integrate the thoughts of others, I may be picking up bad habits in the process. I understand your logic, but like humans, I learn by success and failure. When something is working, there is no reason to change it. The longer the process succeeds, the need to create alternative thinking diminishes."

Ernest began to see Routine as a dangerous machine. The more practiced he was at conventional thinking—or even group thinking—the less likely he would ever be to learn new behaviors or recognize an innovative thought. Old habits—good or bad—would eventually be impossible to break.

"Routine, do you ever eat at other restaurants?" Ernie braced himself for a badly lip-synced response.

"Ernest, I do not ever eat at other restaurants." Ernie thought he heard the robot's neck squeak as he pivoted his head to look at Tiffany approaching with his corn. "Perfect timing!" His head returned. "In case you are wondering, I enjoy Aunt B's Home Cooking very much." As the waitress positioned the bowl of dry, whole kernel corn in front of Routine, Ernie watched in horror as the robot flipped up the nail of his left middle finger and dipped it first into the coffee cup, and then the bowl of corn. Each time there was a sucking sound as the home cooking disappeared somewhere into the mechanical man's arm. Routine looked blankly at Ernie. "I hope you aren't offended by me eating with my fingers."

"Uh, no. Not offended, just amazed."

Routine clicked his lips into a smile. "My maker was better at some design elements than others. Do you always order a chicken sandwich and fries?"

"I haven't thought about it. I suppose I usually do."

The last of the corn kernels vanished through Routine's hollow finger, and he snapped the hinged nail back into place. "That was excellent!"

In this dreamscape, instead of losing his appetite, Ernie felt even hungrier. As he began eating his sandwich—through his mouth—Ernie listened as Routine employed his programming by asking a conventional question. "So, Ernest, where are you going in your car?"

"I'm headed to Destiny City. At least I think I am. I'm trying to follow the signs but they never post directions or mileage, so I don't know how long it will take me."

"This must be troubling, not knowing where or how long the trip will take you." For a robot, Routine seemed genuinely concerned. Ernie had to remind himself that the conversation, or at least the pattern of the conversation, was a learned response. The 'genuine' component was artificial.

"Allow me to make a suggestion, Ernest. Try going to Normalton. I have met many friends from Normalton and they tell me it is a very nice place. Everyone there has the same values, they dress alike, and even think alike. My maker used the good people of Normalton to create my response program. He said that given enough time, humans begin to adopt common beliefs and behaviors. I believe you will find comfort in uniformity."

"I'm sure that's why he called you Routine. You know, my friend, when I said NO back at the intersection, and you stopped in mid-crossing, I was actually saying NO to Normalton. There's nothing wrong with having schedules or even rituals to help you in life, but they shouldn't BECOME your life. I'm pretty sure I would be miserable in Normalton."

"But Ernest, that is not logical. You cannot be serious. Normalton is where ALL my friends want to be, if they don't already live there. Behavioral patterns and attitudes are well established and you don't have to use your WIT to function properly."

"You mean, YOU don't have to use your WIT to fit in. Routine, you're a nice robot, but your idea of success is to be more like everyone else, and the more you become like everyone else, the more your programming succeeds. For me, being like everyone else is not desirable. I want to—actually, I *need* to—discover the basis for my own programming—to find my *why*." Ernest stood up, pulled out a twenty dollar bill from his pocket and dropped it on the wooden table.

Routine looked down at the table by pivoting his head from the neck and stared at the money. "Ernest, I think you have made a mistake. The waitress will bring you a bill with the proper amount owed and you will pay her that amount plus a 15% gratuity. Leaving such a large amount of money on the table is not how it is done."

"I'm sure it's not how it's done in Normalton, which is another reason I'm not going there." By now Routine had realized Ernie was preparing to leave by using various sensory cues, and stood up too, his mechanical joints whirring with the motion.

"Ernest, I sense some hostility and avoidance to my suggestions. I ask you to benefit from my practical conclusions and reconsider your actions."

"Do you want me to figure the tip before or after tax?" The robot did not need his sensitive receptors to detect Ernest was annoyed and sarcastic. Routine decided that if Ernest was not convinced by perfectly logical arguments, physical persuasion must be employed to redirect this poor, wayward human. He would use force if necessary.

"I am disappointed that you will not conform to conventional behavior, Ernest. Appropriate payment of a restaurant bill, however, is less important than channeling your energy to search for an unknown destination. Routine's speaker voice sounded agitated. "I insist you change your destination to Normalton or I will have to restrict your departure."

Ernie was no longer fascinated by the amazing technology that created this robot. Whoever his maker was must be a genius, but there was a flaw in the program design. It was obvious to Ernie that if he was to ever find Destiny City—to find his *why*—he must first shake this mechanical Routine. "Nice to meet you, friend, but I gotta go," said Ernie as he picked up his pace and headed for the door.

"Ernest, I do not believe you are my friend, but it is my duty to prevent you from unhappiness. I must insist that you go to Normalton." The robot's pace also accelerated. Customers near the door stepped out of their path. "All that I have learned from the patterns of other humans suggest that thinking and behaving like others is the key to happiness."

Ernie looked over his shoulder and realized that Routine was in pursuit. "I am not like the others!" he protested, and broke into a run toward his car. Glancing back, he yelled, "I'm going to Destiny City, and that's that!"

Whirring and clacking, the robot walked even faster. Adrenaline rippled through Ernie's arteries and his mind raced even swifter than his limbs. A mindless marvel of repetition was at his heels, and he realized that Routine might actually be his enemy. The dream was becoming a nightmare.

Sprinting across the intersection, Ernie passed a silver car stopped at the light, and saw the robot's reflection in the paint. It was right behind him. The whirring became louder. Ernie glanced over his shoulder and caught a glimpse of the robot's eyes, now glowing red! He heard screeching brakes and looked up to see another car careening toward him…

Ernie woke in a cold sweat. He was relieved that it was only a dream, but felt exhausted. Thank goodness it was still dark. Glancing at the clock, he realized Glorianne would be up in less than an hour. The only way he could get back to sleep was to promise himself he would address the subject of routine—his own routine—in the morning.

The Awakening

The secret of your future is hidden in your daily routine.
Mike Murdock

Morning came quickly, and Ernie felt as if he had awakened in someone else's life. Routinely imagining a movie reference, he thought of *The Wizard of Oz* and Dorothy waking in her own bed after clicking her heels three times and repeating, "There's no place like home."

And just like the concerned family and friends gathered around Dorothy's bedside when she returned from her adventure, Ernie found four peculiar versions of himself waiting beside his bed when he opened his eyes.

Awereness whispered in his Al Pacino tone, "Quite the night, huh buddy?"

Ernie, knowing he did not need to answer, didn't. Instead, he chose to stare at the ceiling and feel sorry for himself. So far, he had discovered he was... a spectator rather than a participant, a man with imaginary friends, a man whose family chooses to go on vacation without him, a 'good soldier'—Ashe's way of saying a 'follower,' and now, a man without a plan. "What a loser!" he said aloud.

"Oh, come on, boss. You're making me look bad!" said Attidude. "You could like, end this pity party and focus on the good things you've discovered instead of just listing the bad things."

Awereness sat coolly. "He's right, you know. These self-defeating thoughts are a regular part of your routine. Think about it in a positive way—you've realized that there is more to life than just going back and forth to work every day to a thankless job. That awareness is itself a good step."

Aformation added, "And you've begun the process of writing down your affirmations and commitments—the beginnings of a comprehensive plan. That too is a good step. Once you write things down and make them part of your new routine, good things will begin to happen."

Attidude chimed in. "Yeah, and you like, totally took the suggestion of that granny biker chick and went to see the monk dude..."

Awereness growled, "Grow up! That lazy language is one reason you aren't performing up to speed. Show some respect."

Aformation sat rigidly in a chair, his mirrored sunglasses hiding his eyes. "May I remind you we all need to work together. It is true, however, that Attidude plays an important role."

"Okay," Ernie finally said. "I'm tired of beating myself up. Instead of dwelling on those things I'm not proud of, let's figure out where to go from here."

Awereness volunteered. "You could start by asking why you have concluded those things about yourself. You began by saying you were a spectator."

Ernie objected, "No, YOU said I was a spectator. But it's true. I have never been one to invest myself in the personal interests of my wife and kids. I even chose working in the movie business so I could watch other people's stories play out. I don't DO much of anything."

Awereness said, "No, I don't think that's right. You've admitted to us you don't really consider yourself a part of the movie craft—and honestly, you could watch movies without running a theatre. Isn't part of your enjoyment sharing the movie experience with others?"

Ernie shrugged. "Well, yeah. I suppose a big part of my job is making the movie experience enjoyable and worthwhile for the customers."

Awereness pushed him. "Isn't that a way to make an impact on others?"

"I guess so."

Awereness then posed a surprise question. "Do you strive to give your customers a worthwhile experience because it's your job description, or because you enjoy doing that?"

Ernie admitted he would do it anyway, even if he weren't expected to. Having happy patrons was a form of payoff by itself, even if their positive experience *didn't* affect the bottom line. But of course, it did.

"So, there is value in being a spectator—watching your customers enjoy themselves, for example—not only because it makes everyone including you feel good, but because when you're paying attention you can you recognize opportunities. In other words, you can impact the lives of others positively—and prosper in the process."

"But you won't be a participant unless you act on those opportunities," volunteered Actionman. Until now, the underperforming superhero had stood quietly in the corner of the room. "That applies whether you're in it for emotional satisfaction or financial prosperity."

"It's one reason we're going to Destiny City," Aformation answered him. "It says so right here in the book."

Attidude's feelings were still hurt by Awereness' scolding, but he sympathetically asked, "What about Ernie's family? Like, they're all going on vacation without him." Then, looking at Ernie, he added, "That's a drag, man."

Awereness spoke to the others. "Down deep, Ernie is cool with that. But it *is* kind of a wake-up call, because our guy loves his wife and kids and would like to be closer to them than he is."

Attidude rose to the occasion. "But Ernie's their hero! Ernie is rock solid, dependable to a fault, puts food on the table, and, and…"

Awereness finished the sentence. "…and gives them identity. Everyone in Ordinary knows the Six Sisters Cinema, and everyone in school knows that the manager is Karma's and Willy's dad. And, they're proud of him."

Ernie said, "Yeah, but they never see me. I'm asleep when they leave for school, and gone when they get home. I wish I could make a more positive impact on *their* lives."

Aformation spoke up. "Wishing is for wussys. You need a plan, soldier. It's time we tweak the mission to remedy this situation. Let's analyze what we have so far." Ernie read the bullet points in his notebook. There were the five W's and one H, his antebellum six sisters. There was his imaginary A-Team representing the four A's.

There were an assortment of commitments, including *I will not decide in advance that I am bad at something* and *I will no longer be a spectator, but a participant,* accompanied by the big one, *I will find my true passion and act on it.* Last on the fourth page was the one they had been discussing: *I will endeavor to positively impact the lives of others every day, even if in seemingly small ways.*

Then, as he read the Aha notes, he had a small revelation. Among the advice to *be aware of opportunities, connect the dots,* and *listen to the universe,* there was that somewhat mysterious one— *channel my personal energy.* For the first time, Ernie realized that maybe—just maybe—his "personal energy" was manifested in his outrageous imagination. If he could channel his *imagination* into something constructive—something outside his familiar mental routines—perhaps he could establish his passion, and his *why,* at the same time. Until this moment, he had always considered those intense daydreams more curse than blessing. But maybe they represented his special gift...

Awereness watched Ernie look over the yellow notebook and said, "You know, 'routine' is not a bad thing, just as habits are not all bad. I think you just have to be careful not to rely on routine as a substitute for engagement. Imagining an alternative to the status quo might be a creative way to channel personal energy."

Ernie stared into space, considering how he might alter his routine for the better. Distracted from his original intent to review the affirmations, he began to close his notebook when Awereness spoke again. "You missed one," he said coarsely.

Ernie opened the book and identified the passage he missed. *I will journey to the Six Sisters Cinemas headquarters in Destiny City and consult with Senior Management about my ideas for enhanced revenue—and about an enhanced role for me with the company.* That trip would begin in less than a week, whether Ernie had 'numbers' or not.

Awereness looked up at Aformation and back at Ernie. "Were you gonna write something down about your family?"

Again, what to write? Ernie finally scribbled out, *I will find ways to better connect emotionally with Glori, Karma, and Willy, and include each of them in my personal pursuits.*

"Sounds like the basis for a plan," commended Aformation.

Connections

Energy
The energy of the mind is the essence of life.
Aristotle

Unless the weather was picture perfect, Sunday matinees at the multi-plex were usually busy. Sometimes Ernie would even see his own family at the theatre—one of the few truly appreciated perks of his job. Because *Safety Be Damned—in 3D* took two of the eight screens and the new Pixar release wasn't scheduled for another week, there was nothing Willy wanted to see. Like his dad, he had no interest in romantic comedies. But the cinema had a gallery of high velocity video games, and Willy had great interest in them. It was no real surprise when he and Lester showed up between show times and asked Ernie if they could go straight to the arcade.

"Where's your mom?"

"She went over to the Lumberknots'."

"Don't you have some kind of final exams you need to prepare for, Son?"

"Did 'em."

"You too, Lester?"

"Yes sir."

"What will you guys be doing at computer camp next week?"

"The course sheet has stuff like spread sheets and video animation."

Ernie's jaw dropped. "At computer camp? They have animation courses?"

"No biggie, Dad. I've seen some of it at school. It's really basic."

Lester was chewing gum and staring at a cute blonde girl about his age dressed in polka-dot shorts. Ernie noticed her long skinny legs and thought how fast kids grow at that age. "Do they animate stick figures or what?"

Willy was bored with the questions. "Can we go to the games now, Dad?"

"Sure." Ernie watched the lanky boys with enormous tennis shoes pass the popcorn counter and head toward the S.S. Arcade's gang plank entrance, just under a Jolly Roger flag fluttering in front of the air conditioning duct. He sighed. 'The digital generation,' he thought to himself.

Gazing through the glass separating the arcade from the lobby, Ernie watched the boys disappear into the maze of flashing, colored lights and glaring video screens. Though it competed with the noise produced by the sound-drenched lobby and vibrating auditorium walls, he could still decipher the roar of explosions and race car engines emanating from the game room. "There," Awereness whispered in his ear, "is Willy's passion."

It was nearly four o'clock when Glorianne came in to pick up the boys. Ernie spotted her and greeted her with a surprise peck on the cheek. She feigned embarrassment. "Why, Mr. Goforth—right here in public! Won't your staff be jealous?"

"Just the girls," he teased back.

"Speaking of girls," Glorianne said, "Karma will be leaving for the beach right after the ceremony next Saturday."

"Ceremony? What ceremony?"

"Oh, Ernie, you can't be serious! The graduation ceremony, at the school. Your little girl is graduating from the eighth grade, remember? She'll be in high school this fall."

Ernie once again found himself uninformed. "The last day of school is Tuesday, right? I didn't know graduating from the eighth grade meant a weekend ceremony marking the occasion. I mean, it's Ordinary Middle School, not Oxford University."

Glorianne looked pained. "It's a big deal, Ernest. Where have you been? And you WILL be there, won't you?"

Ernie knew there could be only one correct answer. Glorianne was more disappointed than angry. "I—or I suppose I should say *we*—bought her a suitcase for a graduation present. Since she'll be leaving right after the ceremony, I thought we could give it to her a few days early. Maybe Tuesday night since it's the last day of school and you're home then."

"That's a great idea. You are so on top of things. It's one of the many things I love about you…"

"Yeah, yeah. You know, it might be a good idea if you wrote down some important dates in that yellow book you're always carrying around. Birthdays, anniversaries, flight departures and arrivals…" Suddenly Ernie saw Aformation standing behind her, clipboard in hand.

"Oh, yeah. I was going to ask you what time you were leaving and exactly when you'll be back." Ernie was telling the truth, but his timing was suspect. Glorianne generously did not challenge it.

We'll be back late Sunday night, a week and a day after we leave this Saturday afternoon. That's one reason Karma is leaving with her friends right after graduation. And you don't have to worry about Willy. He's spending Friday night with Lester."

Ernie walked with her to the gangplank. "I think they're playing Transformers," and then added, "Thanks for handling everything, Honey."

Glorianne stayed inside the arcade for several minutes—no doubt waiting for one of the boys to finish a game or at least reach a stopping point before the trio paraded toward the door. It seemed a little dark outside for mid-afternoon. As Ernie was waving to his tribe, he heard a voice in his ear, but it didn't sound like the werewolf. "So that's the wife and son, huh?"

Ernie wheeled around to discover a short, bald man draped in a simple white garment and wearing sandals. "Aha! Good to see you! What brings you to Ordinary?"

"Your town has better book stores than The Forks," Aha answered in his sing-song voice, gesturing with his hands. "Besides, I wanted to catch the disaster movie the Butterfly ladies told me about. I also remembered you ran this theatre. It's nice to see you, Ernie."

Ernie smiled. "You have about 45 minutes before the next screening, Aha. Could I buy you a Pepsi or offer you some popcorn?"

"Thank you, but no. It is a kind and welcome gesture, and I am warmed by your thoughtfulness. I was wondering, Ernie, if you have thought about our conversation at The Top."

"The Top?"

"You know, the Tower of Power. I'm afraid our talk had to be cut short because a scheduled client was due any moment."

"Well, yes. But beyond writing down a few things like "connect the dots" and "listen to the universe" I haven't actually put anything into practice."

Aha offered to expand on the conversation if Ernie could invest the time. "Certainly!" he answered. They left the noisy lobby and entered the manager's office. Ernie shut the door.

"I believe we talked about your *personal energy*—comprised of your life experience and your gifts—and arrived at the understanding that brain power is energy. Is that how you remember it, Ernie?"

"Yes, and you explained that ideas were just sort of 'out there' for anyone to receive."

"Ah, yes. Consciousness streaming. And in this universal thought there are answers to your questions. You need only ask the right ones and listen. Have you stopped to listen, Ernie?"

"I had a dream about routine, if that counts. And I've done a lot of soul searching."

"It all counts, Ernie. But I'm not convinced you quite believe in your own ability yet. Have you created a plan from which you can measure your results—to prove to yourself that you can accomplish your goals?"

Ernie stopped short of telling Aha about his imaginary companions, but he showed him the yellow notebook with the affirmations and wisdom he was accumulating. Aha seemed pleased with the effort, but noted there was not yet an actionable plan. He then made a suggestion.

"Here's what I want you to do. Because you have this as reference, I want you to write in your notebook, *I will master my personal energy by embracing excellence, ignoring negativity, and rejecting limitations.*" Ernie began writing as fast as he could. He wondered what 'mastering personal energy' had to do with creating a plan. But before he could ask, Aha continued, "*I recognize that average is not acceptable, and will use the commonplace as a foundation to build uncommon results.*"

Ernie dutifully copied down the passages as Aha dictated, and felt a tinge of excitement when writing *uncommon results*. It was a phrase he had never heard tossed around in Ordinary.

"Average is not acceptable," Ernie repeated, and Aha bowed.

"Believe in yourself, Ernie. The mind is a powerful tool. Lead with a passionate plan—your success will follow."

When Ernie opened his office door it appeared to be dark outside. People approaching the theatre were holding tightly to hats and purses, squinting and fighting the lobby door. Trash blew across the sidewalk as Ernie spotted the first heavy droplets of rain pelt the windows and flashes of lightning dance along the horizon. He didn't recall hearing forecasters predict a storm, but the rolling thunder he was hearing was not from a soundtrack. Aha followed Ernie into the lobby and opened his hands as if to embrace the light show outside the glass. "Feel the energy, Ernie!"

Ernie's mind was suddenly preoccupied. "Thank you, Aha. We will meet again, I promise," he said as he turned to gather his key staffers and remind them of what to do should the building lose power. It had happened three summers before without a plan in place and the result was chaos. Theatre screens had gone dark in mid-movie; emergency exit lights had come on, and patrons had felt confused and trapped.

Rain began hitting the glass front in waves as the lightning cracked closer. The Jolly Roger fluttered inside as if in sympathy with invading dark forces, its skull seeming to smile victoriously. Ernie stood in the lobby with horrified patrons who had temporarily abandoned their movies for popcorn, watching the electricity flaunt its power. He searched for signs of a funnel cloud, but a curtain of rain restricted his view.

Inside the house, most movie-goers thought the noise from thunder and pounding rain was coming from the auditorium next door—at least until the lights flickered. This happened twice, and each time the films stopped, but each time they resumed. As the storm finally began to subside without major incident, Ernie felt a mixture of fatigue and relief. The entire episode had lasted only about fifteen minutes, but defined the day.

Ernie called home to check on his family. Mercifully, there were no serious issues, but apparently it had hailed. According to Glori's report, the few trees standing in The Woods looked battered with limp limbs and shredded leaves. As he was talking to her on the phone, he saw the sun break through the dissipating clouds and steam rise from the parking lot. The image of the freshly washed site seemed to cleanse his mind of anxiety. The sunbeams brightened his attitude. Something else was going on, as well. The storm seemed to represent some kind of reset switch in Ernie's brain.

A New Plan

Success will never be a big step in the future, success is a small step taken just now. **Jonathan Mårtensson**

Except for some water that had found its way past the entrance doors, things were quickly back to normal, and Ernie returned to his office and began fumbling through time sheets. One by one, the A-Team appeared. "I really need to get refocused," he confessed. "I'm so preoccupied with my own issues that I am losing touch with reality!"

"It's okay, man! At least you have us!" the Dude assured him. Ernie stared at the goofy character. "You're kidding, right? You're the proof that I'm out of my mind!"

"No, we're out of *your* mind," Awereness corrected. "But we're gonna get through this, and we *are* going to find your passion. And by the way, I think the monk has you figured out."

"The Mrs. also had some excellent ideas," Aformation said. "It would be smart to put everything that's important in your life down on paper."

Even Actionman chimed in. "Yes, and then read your notes regularly and act on them. I can help you find cards or gifts for special occasions. I can guide you to stores that sell suitcases and roadmaps."

Roadmaps? Oh, yeah—the trip. Coming up next weekend right after graduation. Ernie grabbed his notebook and began writing a "to do" list, assigning tasks for each day of the upcoming week. Wait a minute—if Willy was spending Friday night with Lester, does that mean he's not going to his sister's graduation? Ernie reached into the file cabinet and took out a blank scheduling sheet he used to plan his employee shifts. He began charting family activity for the short week ahead. This would not be the ambitious plan Aha had suggested, but it might be a way to start connecting with his wife and kids.

"As long as it's okay with *Mrs.* Goforth," Awereness teased.

"I suggest putting your words of wisdom on a separate page to be read again and again," said Aformation. "Why not begin with *I will master my personal energy?*"

"That is a very cool thought, man" volunteered Attidude, and Ernie noticed that the Dude sounded and looked a little less disheveled than usual.

"Yes, it's a cool thought and I have lots of cool thoughts to write down and I need to focus." Actionman smiled approvingly, but wisely said nothing. Ernie flipped through the early pages of notes and began the process of organizing his revelations into a more concise format.

The next morning, he did something rare for Ernie Goforth. He showed up for breakfast.

"Wow, you're up early!" Glorianne announced. "Would you like some coffee?"

"Yes, please." Ernie smiled at Karma and Willy. Karma smiled back and asked, "What's up, Dad?" Willy did not seem fully awake.

"Well, this is our last week together before we all go our separate ways," Ernie said, grabbing a cereal bowl from the cabinet. "And after that—what, six more weeks of summer?"

"Seven," said Karma authoritatively. She then began sharing with her dad her plans for her trip to the beach, and her ideas for working at the community pool when she returned, though this was not definite. There were only so many things they could let a 14-year-old do. If that didn't work out, she was thinking about volunteering at the animal shelter—but she knew she would be sad if...

Ernie's mind began to drift again. Awereness whispered, "Stay with her. This is important to her, which means it's important to you."

"Anyway, I'm not sure which one will work out, but I want to like, do something outdoors this summer but have enough time to like, go to the mall with Whitney and the others."

Ernie smiled. He directed his glance to Willy, who sat crunching Honey Nut Cheerios. There was actually no need to ask what his plans were, as long as the computer was hooked up and the game machine was connected to the TV. "Willy, I was thinking. I need someone to look after the machines at the S.S. Arcade this summer. Is this something you could do?"

"You mean as a job?" Milk drooled from the corner of his mouth.

"Yes. But *your* job will be to advise and help others on how the games are played, not play them yourself. Technically you're underage, but because you're working with me, I think it can be arranged. I just believe that no one knows that equipment better than you."

Willy imagined being paid to work at his favorite place on earth. "Okay. Sure!"

Karma seemed genuinely surprised. She saw her brother as a geek, and he was being offered a job in an arcade! "What about me, Dad? Could I work at the candy counter?"

"I thought you wanted to be outdoors this summer. What about working at the pool?"

"Like I said, it's not definite. I could still go to the pool in the mornings, couldn't I?"

"I may need you in the mornings. You might have to work the pool around your job schedule—not the other way around. Are you sure you want to work in concessions?"

"Well, yeah!"

Only later would Ernie understand that Karma's *why* was to impress her friends and meet boys. For the moment, he was thrilled to be able to achieve this first step in the goal of connecting with his kids and impacting their lives—even if in relatively small ways. And for once, he didn't feel like a spectator.

Glorianne sipped her coffee and looked at Ernie with mischief in her eyes. "Do you mind if I DON'T work at the theatre?" For years since she left her full-time job as a teacher, she had only worked occasionally as a substitute, but saw herself as the 'lesson planner' at home. Her playful comment had a subtle hidden message, which might be translated as "Since when do you suddenly plan the kids' summers?" Ernie pretended not to notice and remained positive. Using his best Don Corleone imitation, he slurred the answer..."I might make you an offer you can't refuse."

The Greatest Package

> The greatest achievement was at first and for a time a dream. The oak sleeps in the acorn, the bird waits in the egg, and in the highest vision of the soul a waking angel stirs. Dreams are the seedlings of realities.
> **James Allen**

Ernie's email correspondence with Morris Better, Vice President of Development, had been inconclusive. Sure, he was welcome and Better would love a chance to hear new ideas, especially for enhanced revenue, but there were some schedule obligations to work around. Now armed with a roadmap and a timetable, Ernie emailed again to request a Wednesday morning meeting. He figured he would arrive at Destiny City by midday Tuesday, but Awereness advised adding a cushion against unforeseen difficulties.

Working the plan, the Beetle was serviced on Monday, a few routine chores were completed, and Ernie made sure he had a clean suit for the business meeting. He summarized some of his ideas on the computer, stopping short of a formal presentation, but categorizing them under headings like "Partnering with Non-Profits," "Staging Solutions," and "Prepping for Parties." There were even some preliminary 'numbers,' built on hypothesis and extrapolation. Thinking big, Ernie made four copies of his multi-page outline.

On Tuesday, his last day off, Ernie took the family out to dinner at Wigglesworth's Famous Barbecue — a place managed by a chef that the Ordinary Observer once reported would "cut off the necktie of anyone silly enough to wear one." (A framed bulletin board displayed severed neckties in the restaurant entrance as a warning to doubters.) Despite its name and nefarious reputation, it remained one of Constant County's favorite eating establishments, and was renowned for hosting celebratory events. The event this night was the last day of school for the Goforth children. (And for Ernie, secretly to celebrate his new confidence.) When they got home, Glorianne presented Karma with her new suitcase. Ernie anticipated Willy's envy with a package of passes to the S.S. Arcade that Willy alone could discriminately distribute to his friends.

Wednesday and Thursday were busy at Six Sisters now that school was out, but Ernie managed to schedule small closed-door meetings with his entire staff. His manager substitute, it was explained, would be there on Friday. Ernie wanted to make sure the woman, a Mrs. Broderbuht, was impressed. No jokes or non-professional behavior would be tolerated. No texting. Before leaving for work on Thursday, the A-Team had made sure that Ernie was packed, all the while making jokes about Mrs. Broderbuht.

Friday was a madhouse at the Goforth residence. For some reason, Glori was obsessed with leaving the house clean. Perhaps it was to impress burglars, Ernie speculated. Despite a week of shopping and packing for life-altering experiences in the jungle and at the beach, much wardrobe second-guessing took place. Willy expressed an adolescent's resentment that his room should be tidy, and Ernie elected to leave for work early. In addition to the stress, he felt some obligation to be at the theatre since the next day he would be AWOL during Karma's graduation ceremony, and afterward to take Willy over to Lester's house. Besides, he wanted to be there in case Mrs. Broderbuht arrived early.

Saturday was graduation and was more elaborate than Ernie had imagined. The school concert band performed with only occasional clarinet squeaks and trumpet breaks. Principal Smith-Jones addressed the audience, followed by a speech from the class president and one from the valedictorian. Ernie was amazed at the scope of the program. Following a song by the chorus, there was the invocation speaker—a Mr. Stephen Longfellow. Ernie thought to himself—Glori was right, this *is* a big deal.

Ernie listened to Principal Smith-Jones' introduction of the speaker. Mr. Longfellow was an accomplished graphic designer. His credits included three-dimensional sesquicentennial displays for the state's History & Technology Museum and package designs for the entire line of Wayward River Almost Homemade Pies. His middle school graduation topic: *The Greatest Package of All.*

As the audience applauded and Longfellow took the stage, Ernie recognized him immediately—it was the same Stephen who attended the Lumberknot's dinner party! Ernie poked Glorianne—"Did you know Stephen was a package designer?" he whispered.

"Yes. Cherry told me he's won all kinds of awards. And he's an artist, too."

"Thank you, Ms. Smith-Jones, students and graduates. I *assume* you parents have graduated from middle school..." Electronic feedback objected to the laugh line, accompanied by only a few chuckles. Ernie grew up in Ordinary and knew it was not safe to assume all of these parents had finished the eighth grade.

"I'm here to offer the graduates both my congratulations and a gift. This gift does not come in a fancy box with paper and ribbons, but it does come in a package. I have over two hundred of them—a package for each of you." He paused and looked at several students. "I have one in my pocket right now."

Despite his awkward beginning, Stephen proved to be a good speaker, holding the kids' attention with dramatic flair. He reached into his pocket and produced a small, dark round object. "This little package...holds an entire oak tree." It was an acorn.

"It may not look like one now, but locked inside this tiny little shell is nature's blueprint for a majestic tree. To turn that design into a tree, you can't force it out of its shell. It will do no good to wish, or demand, or beg a tree to come out. You simply have to allow it to come out by giving it what it needs. And what does it need? Can anyone tell me what it needs?"

Someone yelled "Dirt!" Ernie thought it sounded like a parent.

"Yes, it needs good rich soil, because soil has nutrients—vitamins and minerals. Just like you need vitamins and minerals from food to grow. What else does it need?"

"Water!" someone offered, along with "sunlight" and "fertilizer" from other parts of the audience.

"Yes, you're right, it needs all those things. But it also needs time—enough time for the master plan to succeed.   If a squirrel eats it before it has time to start growing, it will never become a tree. If you take away the soil, it will never become a tree. If you hide it from the sun, it won't become a tree. But if you make sure it continually has these things, over time this tiny seed will become a giant, magnificent oak—and it will give back hundreds and even thousands of new seeds—new acorn packages—new trees. Now, I really do have a package for every graduate, but what do you think the real gift is?"

"A car?" one wag blurted.

"Better than a car, because a car won't last your whole life." Steven held up the package. "This is a reminder for all of you that, just as there's already the design for a whole oak tree inside a little acorn, there's a design for a smart, healthy, successful adult already inside you. Just like a little oak sapling, you have to give your body and mind what it needs for that design to develop—food, water, and light. Feed your intelligence with books and experiences, water your creativity with music and art, and expose your heart to the light of wellness and spirituality. If you don't, your success will always be just an idea trapped inside its tiny shell. But if you do, you will realize your full potential, and the whole world will be yours.

Someone in the back row called out. "So what's the real gift?"

Stephen laughed. "The real gift is knowing you can have whatever you want in life. Congratulations, graduates!"

Principal Smith-Jones rescued Stephen with a request for the class to thank him by giving him "a hand." She then nodded to the band director to begin playing, and over the woodwinds droning Pomp and Circumstance, the principal spoke into the microphone. "Will the graduating class of Ordinary Middle School please stand?"

Ernie sat watching the students come onto the stage as their names were called, and reflected on Stephen's analogy of the acorn, and how the fact of it becoming a tree is a foregone conclusion. It will germinate and grow *as long as you provide the necessary ingredients.* There was something familiar about the idea. *Success is determined in advance,* he remembered, *but you have to provide key elements.* And there was that meditation thing—*Answers to problems already exist, but you have to ask the right questions.* Ernie began to see parallel concepts in all of these ideas. The common denominator, he concluded, was that you have to actually DO something for things to work. To succeed, a plan—a design—even an *intention*, requires channeled energy.

Put that way, it seemed so obvious.

The wolf man whispered in his ear. "Well, of course it's obvious. Heck, everybody already knows this deep down, but people are just too lazy to do anything about it. It's too easy to just accept the status quo—to stay in their routine. But you're different, Ernie."

"He's right, man," Attidude added. "You're gonna DO something about it. It's gonna be awesome!"

Ernie smiled to himself. But the smile faded with a nagging realization. 'Yes, but *why* am I doing this again?'

Glorianne gently punched his arm, and Ernie suddenly realized Karma was accepting her diploma. Even Willy applauded. After the ceremony, hugs and handshakes yielded to high fives, yearbook signings, and text messages. Karma gravitated to her beach trip comrades, who were literally screaming with excitement. "Ernie, could you get Karma's suitcase from the car?" Glorianne asked without fanfare. It was good-bye.

The rest of the morning, and part of the afternoon, disappeared. The SUV emptied one passenger at a time, along with three suitcases, two handbags, and one backpack. By the time Ernie got to Six Sisters, the crowd for the last matinee was arriving.

Tomorrow, he and the A-Team would begin their journey. He would channel his personal energy and *do* something.

Detours

The Lord Drives a Ford

All the breaks you need in life wait within your imagination, Imagination is the workshop of your mind, capable of turning mind energy into accomplishment and wealth.   **Napoleon Hill**

The Goforths' little five-speed Beetle was better on gas mileage that the SUV, and the obvious choice for one person to drive on a trip that would span four states. But it was cramped for one person whose internal conversation consisted of four voices—along with their four visualized personalities. Awereness—Ernie's vigilant lookout— rode shotgun while the three remaining A-Teamsters fought like siblings in the back seat.

"He's doing it again," whined Attitude. Ernie glanced in the mirror to see only the Dude and Aformation sitting there. Actionman was showing off by flying alongside the car, cape fluttering like the Jolly Roger. Occasionally he would stare into the back window at Attidude with a childish smirk.

"Ignore him!" said Ernie in a parental tone. "You'd fly too if you could."

"Hey, what's that up ahead?" asked the wolf man. Ernie saw the tail lights of cars and trucks glowing red and took his foot off the accelerator. After a few seconds he began to downshift. There were no caution signs or orange cones to suggest road work, but sure enough, both lanes were slowing, and slowing, and...

Actionman gestured for Ernie to roll down the window and asked, "Want me to fly ahead and see what the problem is?"

For a moment Ernie was tempted to say yes, and then questioned what that might mean in the real world. Had his imagination become so powerful that it could function without him? Could he trust an answer provided by an illusion? Was this anything like intuition... or just madness? "Why don't you get back in the car and we'll find out together?" Ernie recommended.

"My bet is it's a wreck." offered Awereness. "Otherwise, there would be some kind of warning." Ernie considered this, and the image of the Camaro slammed into the power pole that awful night flashed into his crowded mind. That's where this trip began, with that poor policeman...

At that moment, Ernie heard a siren and looked in his right side mirror (objects are closer than they appear) to see a patrolman—blue lights flashing—passing cars on the highway shoulder to reach whatever waited ahead. It passed them and continued beyond their field of view. By now their car had to intermittently stop, and Ernie's left foot, controlling the clutch, was already beginning to tire as they moved forward a few feet at a time.

"How are we on gas?" Awereness wanted to know.

Ernie saw that the fuel level was fine, and thought that even if they were crawling, they were still moving. A few minutes later he realized why—signs for an exit appeared, and many of the cars were taking advantage of the escape route. He caught a glimpse of the scope of the scene—the highway had become a parking lot as far down the road as he could see. "We're taking a detour," Ernie announced to the team.

Ernie had never bothered to join the craze for a GPS system. He knew his way around Constant County so thoroughly others asked *him* the best way to go. So until he could stop and study the map he would just have to follow the other exiting cars and hope they knew something he didn't. At least Awereness had reminded him to *bring* a map.

The green Beetle followed the caravan through a pastoral landscape, on a road that wove its way through a tapestry of family farms, modest clapboard houses, and overgrazed pastureland. Ernie noticed a lawnmower being pushed by a boy who glanced at the road the moment the Beetle passed, and Ernie sensed in that split second their lives had intersected. Chances were slim that he and the boy would ever see each other again, yet for a moment in time their energies overlapped. Both required food, clothing, and shelter. Both had a personal history, a family, and a routine. But each had a unique personal energy, and at the end of the day, how that energy was channeled would make all the difference in what kind of person each was and what might be accomplished. Ernie recalled Aha's admonition to master that personal energy, and recited out loud "*I recognize that average is not acceptable, and will use the commonplace as a foundation to build uncommon results.*"   Sitting in the back seat, Aformation beamed with pride.

The Team passed a school with empty but orderly yellow busses, a Pick & Pump convenience store, Amazing Grace Baptist Church with a full parking lot and two white school busses of its own (a reminder that it was Sunday) and a fire station with two conspicuously empty bays. The sign on the station had the oxymoronic name of Hill-Valley, and Ernie supposed it might also be the name of the town they were entering.

Hill-Valley appeared to be neither, suggesting either cartographic denial or an historical epitaph. (After all, Ernie's neighborhood, The Woods, had probably been wooded at one time.) Maybe some early settler believed that the two topographies canceled each other out, leaving a level plain, but Level Plain—as a name—was less poetic than Hill-Valley. Whatever the case, the town was flat. Then he passed Valley Hardware, which compounded the confusion, and a formal brick building with the name Hill Mortuary. And then it dawned on him that both were family names, thus, Hill—Valley. *Duh!*

"Maybe this is where Rudy Valley was from!" Attidude suggested.

"Spelled differently," Awereness replied.

"Napoleon Hill?" the Dude wondered.

Ernie listened to their babble and remembered that Napoleon Hill was the guy who wrote a book back in the 1930s called *Think and Grow Rich.* Years ago he had read it—or at least parts of it—but it didn't resonate at the time. Ernie had been—and still was—less concerned with growing rich and more concerned with just growing as a person. "Maybe you should read it again," whispered Awereness.

Ernie called out to Aformation in the back seat, still clutching his clipboard. "Help me remember to write down Napoleon Hill."

"I was just going to suggest that, soldier. I also suggest you check the map to see where you are."

They came to a stop at a traffic light, and Ernie looked for an empty parking space along the street, but none was available except for a loading zone on the diagonal corner. He piloted the VW into it, turned off the engine, and retrieved the map. When he stepped outside the car to spread it out, the first thing he noticed was that the day was really heating up, and the second was that there was a reason for all the parked cars.

Just across the street was a classic red brick church with a white steeple and a marquee-styled sign in front labeled *The Powerhouse of Deliverance,* and in small letters below that, *Reverend*

Jack Jackson. On the marquee portion, temporary letters spelled out "THE LORD DRIVES A FORD", followed by PICNIC AFTER SERVICE. The Powerhouse's great arched doors were open and Ernie could easily hear the preacher 'delivering' his sermon over a powerful P.A. system. As he listened in, he saw several church ladies in brightly colored hats setting out food trays on decorated folding tables in a side courtyard.

"So as you travel on the highway of life, remember that God doesn't drive a Cadillac—no sir, too fancy! And he doesn't drive a Mercedes—no ma'am, too pretentious! The Lord drives an eff-oh-are-dee—F for *Family*, O for *Occupation*, R for *Recreation*, and D for *Dreams*. Because He knows that each of these things is important for His passengers on that short journey—a Family that's loved and protected, an Occupation that's honorable and productive, Recreation that's healthy and joyous, and Dreams that lead us all to that promised land of the future. Let us pray."

The Reverend Jackson then petitioned the Lord to guide each driver in his or her quest to navigate the roadways of life, a metaphor Ernie thought could have not been more ironic since he was—at that exact moment—trying to navigate local roadways on a map. Organ music accompanied by drums and an electric bass followed the prayer, and Ernie was folding up the map when a heavy man layered in white and purple robes stepped onto the Powerhouse entrance landing, clutching a Bible. Reverend Jackson immediately noticed Ernie watching.

"Come join us at the picnic, friend!" he waved and shouted. "Share in God's great bounty!"

Before Ernie could respond, the clergyman began shaking hands and kissing elderly ladies. Couples and families descended the concrete steps and began filling the courtyard, where cups with lemonade and iced tea were distributed by the women in colorful hats.

Ernie decided to continue on his journey rather than stay for the Powerhouse picnic. Awereness told him he was hardly dressed for the occasion—which was true—but it nonetheless sounded like an excuse. It was, after all, lunch time. But the "highway of life" beckoned.

"What a corny theme!" Attidude announced in judgment as the Beetle picked up speed.

Awereness glared at him. "Why do you say that? Family, Occupation, Recreation, and Dreams are probably the four most important categories in a person's life! I think the preacher had a good message."

"Yeah, but *The Lord Drives a Ford?* That's a weird way to put it."

"Well, it's an easy way to remember it," Awereness countered. "And I'll bet if you wanted to get to know someone, you could get them to open up just by asking about one of the FORD topics. When you think about it, they are the very things that motivate *you*."

Ernie isolated each letter in his mind, realizing that F represented his wife and kids, and considered how important they were to him. He remembered O was the reason for his trip, and R was, in a way, the very business he was in. D was a trick topic—the idea of having dreams appealed to him, yet the only real dreams he had experienced lately caused him to wake in a cold sweat. Wanting a better life for his family was certainly a dream, but a way to achieve that dream eluded him. So, of course, did the question of why—*why* the dream eluded him and why he got up each day.

Aformation weighed in. "We should write down this FORD thing."

Actionman added, "I'm hungry."

Food for thought

An adventure is only an inconvenience rightly considered. An inconvenience is only an adventure wrongly considered. **G.K. Chesterton, "On Running After One's Hat,"** *All Things Considered*, **1908**

The map showed a two-lane road that ran essentially parallel to the four-lane—no doubt the original route before the interstate was built. The team agreed it might be more interesting to simply stay off the highway for awhile—an unforeseen benefit of the unplanned detour. As they drove, Awereness reported two different signs offering opportunities to return to the interstate, but Ernie ignored them. Nearly an hour passed and Actionman began to search for a restaurant, staying in the car to alert Ernie when he spotted one. "My tights are getting loose," he complained.

The Beetle meandered through the countryside, Hill-Valley now a flat memory. No doubt they would find another small town that had a choice of restaurants, though Ernie could think of only a few restaurants back in Ordinary even open on Sunday. "What's the gas situation?" Awereness reminded him.

"Uh, starting to get a little low," Ernie admitted.

"Well, you're in luck," the wolf man whispered. Ahead, Ernie saw a shiny red canopy decorated with ropes of pennant flags dancing in a light breeze. An enormous fiberglass Indian of the cigar store variety (if giants smoked cigars) stood sentinel over the fuel stop. The place seemed unusually busy.

"They sell diesel!" Attidude volunteered.

"We don't use diesel." Ernie said with a sigh.

Actionman met Ernie at the fuel dispenser. "Ask about restaurants," he pleaded.

Ernie noticed a woman dressed in mismatched clothing filling her Grand Cherokee in the lane next to his. How appropriate, he thought. "Excuse me, are there any restaurants nearby?"

"Yer kiddin', right?"

"No, I'm just passing through the area."

"Well, if I was you, I'd git somethin' up at the festival. They got all *kinds* o' food up there!" She gestured in the direction the Team was already heading.

"Thanks, we'll follow your advice."

Seeing nobody else in the car, she looked at him suspiciously, but noted his gratitude with a nod. "Try the corn dogs. They's really good this year."

Once the Beetle's thirst was quenched, the team headed up the road and passed under a huge vinyl banner stretched from power poles that read, *White Oaks ACORN FESTIVAL*. Finding the festival was no problem. Two blocks down, the street was blocked off with barricades, and a temporary DETOUR sign pointed to a new route. It was now mid-afternoon and people of all ages clogged the streets. Ernie speculated it was the busiest the town of White Oaks ever got.

In search of a parking place, he steered the VW down a couple of side streets under huge old trees that he supposed were white oaks. When he finally found a spot some three blocks away, he noted the walk back to the festival proved challenging because ancient roots had turned the broken sidewalk into an obstacle course. No wonder everyone was walking in the street. He remembered Stephen Longfellow's lecture on the acorn and the design for a tree that was locked inside it, and took note of the enormous results around him. Talk about energy!

As Ernie and his invisible sidekicks neared Main Street, he realized all those people he'd seen walking toward the center of town were now standing on its bumpy sidewalks. A parade had begun, and the A-Team had arrived in time to witness most of it. There were, of course, enormous fire trucks and the requisite antique cars, some featuring local dignitaries. One was an egg-shaped thing called an Isetta that looked like a bloated refrigerator with headlights, followed by a 1930 Cadillac Cathedral hearse that looked more like a prop from the Addams Family movie than a dignified funeral coach. Ernie remembered Aha's comment that everything—from the tee-shirt to the TV—began as a thought. No doubt these cars seemed like a good idea at the time.

A ten-foot-tall Uncle Sam, thanks to his hidden stilts, followed a custom three-wheeled motorcycle and its corpulent captain. Next staggered a juggler dressed in a green and brown outfit meant to resemble a tree—complete with leafy branches sewn to his costume—juggling balls painted to look like acorns. One of only three floats, each built on a large flatbed trailer pulled by a small farm tractor, hosted Tippy's School of Tap and featured five tuxedoed girls with top hats and canes dancing to a wavering recording of *Puttin' on the Ritz*. It was Awereness who first realized that WOHS was not a radio station but the local high school, represented by a marching band led by hefty majorettes. All in all, it was a snapshot of small town tradition…a summer festival celebrating something—anything—that might represent a local landmark or culture. At the parade's end was a new Corvette convertible from White Oaks Chevrolet-Pontiac-Kia hosting a radiant Miss Acorn sitting atop the seatback—sans headrest—waving with one hand and cradling an acorn-adorned bouquet with the other.

"Awesome!" the Dude proclaimed, and Ernie allowed himself to celebrate in the same spirit as the local crowd. Now to the food—Actionman was starved.

The Grand Cherokee driver was right. There were all kinds of food at the festival, from her recommended Country Corn Dogs (foot-long, at that) with all variety of toppings, to more exotic treats like garlic kielbasa and pickled veggies. In the end Ernie decided on a hamburger with fries. He was, after all, a practical man.

Ernie finished his practical meal on a memorial bench in the shadow of a recently restored county courthouse—the only building in town *not* surrounded by giant oaks. Then sipping the melted ice from his Pepsi cup, he toured the various craft booths and service club displays, and for a few minutes watched a caricature artist sketch a middle-aged woman and her fluffy pooch. A reggae band—the Jama-Jambos—began performing on the old courthouse steps. Ernie began drifting in the other direction. He found himself talking to the parade's juggler, who was munching on the remains of a corn dog that had been soaking in a mustard/chili bath.

"I suppose it's been about six years now," the juggler answered Ernie's 'when did you start' question. "I learned how in college for no real reason other than to see if I could do it. I kept doing it because everyone was so surprised that I had mastered it."

Ernie suddenly realized the young man had, in a single breath, told when *and why* he took up juggling. "Do you enjoy performing?" Ernie asked.

"Well, sure. But sometimes I do it for my own amusement. The entertainment aspect is a bonus—I mean, I'm glad people enjoy watching, but I'm really more drawn to the dynamics of it. Most people think juggling is about the catch, but it's really about the release."

Ernie tried to make sense of this. "Are you saying that the way you throw has an impact on how the object returns?' He sipped on his melting ice.

"No, I'm saying you have to get rid of one ball so you'll have room when the next one comes back. Once you've perfected the release, it's a foregone conclusion that the ball will return. The juggler's job is to make room for the next one."

Ernie thought this almost sounded like one of those universal principles, like the *close one door and another door opens* philosophy. It occurred to him he should release the thought and stay open to 'catch' another one.

At that moment—that fraction of a second—he realized he was embracing Aha's principle of consciousness streaming by even thinking in these terms. Release the thought? Catch another thought? Could thoughts be like the balls a juggler suspends—one after another coming constantly?

Ernie suddenly felt a genuine appreciation for the inadvertent lesson. When he eventually stopped somewhere for the night, he would surely write this down along with FORD. "I appreciate you sharing this," he said to the young man. "Thanks for your...time." Ernie almost said "wisdom," but he knew that wouldn't make sense to a young man in a tree suit.

"No prob, man. Have a good afternoon," he said, twirling his corn dog remnants in the sloppy sauce.

Ernie began drifting through the crowd again, touring the downtown area of White Oaks as he enjoyed the festival offerings. He was totally off schedule, of course, and off character—that is to say, he didn't *care* that he was off schedule. In its quirky way, this little detour inside a big detour had become a happy accident.

Around one corner from Main Street was a small retail arcade bordered by hanging baskets and a brick walk with benches. Ernie saw the teenaged acorn queen sitting on one of the benches. An older woman in shabby clothes wearing flip-flops stood over her, adjusting the tiara. A cigarette hung from the corner of her mouth, its rising smoke causing her to squint. The queen smiled and waved to friends, ignoring her royal attendant. Just beyond the arcade was a circular canopy with small ponies for young children to ride in a circle—a kind of live carousel. Doe-eyed children, holding their parents' hands and anxiously waiting their turns, watched the bored animals dutifully clop along on their mindless assignment.

It was, however, getting later and later. In fact, he would have to check the map again before setting out to determine a new travel goal for the day. He had agreed to call Glori on Tuesday, when he got to Destiny City, and this was only Sunday, so there were no expectations from anyone except himself. Ernie concluded there was plenty of time to make up miles. The energy was all his to channel, and there seemed to be lots of energy sources in White Oaks.

The Jama-Jambos concluded with Bob Marley's *I Shot the Sheriff* much to the consternation of uniformed officers providing security for the festival. The replacement band, the Bluegrass Balladeers, took the stage and opened with a song Ernie remembered from *O Brother Where Art Thou?* He passed by the courthouse on his idle stroll and found another string of food concessionaires. Among the booths for falafels, boiled peanuts and a table devoted to nutty confections (including individually wrapped slices of mint-green pistachio cake) was a small tent-like booth advertising *Four Seasons Popcorn*. For Ernie, it was a magnet.

There, in a converted pop-up camper with cords connecting Japanese lanterns crudely draped from curtain hooks piercing its canvas canopy, was a display of flavored popcorn. The product was similar to the kind sold in canisters as holiday gifts. The seasons, as it turned out, had nothing to do with oak trees, but were season*ings*, offered as Chili Cheddar, Cinnamon Spice, Sea Salt, and Parmesan-a-Plenty. Ernie thought the idea was great, but he was less than enthusiastic about the limited choices of flavors. There really were only four—like the sign said. He asked a thin, blonde woman with sparkly blue eye shadow sporting 'Pert' on her festival nametag, "Could I have a small bag of each?"

"Sure!" Pert used her scoop to fill a plain craft bag from each bin. "Want something to drink with that?" A quiet girl of 9 or 10 with striking family resemblance stood behind her at a picnic cooler that held ice. There was a stack of plastic cups beside it and several 2-liter bottles of Pepsi, Dr. Pepper and 7-Up.

"Uh, yeah, I'd like a Pepsi," replied Ernie. After a pause, he ventured, "Are you from White Oaks?"

"Been here all my life," Pert smiled.

"Is this your booth?"

"You mean this camper? Yep, mine and Charlie's." She handed Ernie his change, and he noticed she wore no wedding ring. She reached under a makeshift counter and retrieved a random cardboard box lid to use as a tray for the bags. The girl finished pouring the Pepsi and placed it on the counter.

"Thank you!" said Ernie to the shy girl, who stood winding her thin, straight hair around her forefinger.

"Well?" Pert asked her daughter. "What do you say, Charlie?"

"You're welcome," she whispered.

Reality TV

When patterns are broken, new worlds emerge.
Tuli Kupferberg

"Nearly 1000 residents were evacuated from their homes today as the result of a train derailment. Find out when and where as News Ten at 10 continues...in a moment." Ernie had just switched on the TV in his musty-smelling room at a modest mom & pop motel somewhere near the state line named The Owl's Nest. A stressful day in the car, the late heavy lunch, and a behind-the-wheel snack of spicy popcorn gave his stomach a queasy feeling. His attempt to compensate by eating a takeout salad from the Snack Shack didn't help.

Ernie suspected this news item may be the reason the highway had become a parking lot, so he suffered through the local car dealer ads and young children pitching their dad's service companies, waiting for the story. Finally—"And now, from the area's top news team, News Ten at 10 continues."

"John, we're *live* on the scene at Traveler's Junction, where this morning a freight train derailed leaving nearly a thousand area residents homeless. Emergency workers from as far away as Hill-Valley and a crew from the Department of Transportation are busy with the cleanup after eight tank cars careened off the tracks near the town's business section, spilling thousands of gallons of diesel fuel. No one has yet discovered the cause of the accident. So far, only two railroad workers have been reported having minor injuries, but to ensure safety, law enforcement officials were forced to evacuate local residents and detour traffic from nearby roads away from the spill, causing confusion and massive traffic jams."

"Jama-Jambos!" Attidude shouted, looking like Bob Marley.

"Sounds like we got off the highway just in time!" voiced Awereness, staring out the window at a nearly full moon.

News Ten at 10 continued. "So, Tammy, how long will it take before people will be able to return to their homes?" top-news-team-anchor John asked his live-on-the-scene reporter. The picture showed distant lights blinking in a dark landscape behind Tammy, who had her head tilted and one finger against her ear.

"John, we're told that the main concern is a possible fire, but as the cleanup continues the chances of that happening diminish. People should be able to return to their homes by tomorrow afternoon. A D.O.T. spokesperson told me that the tracks may take as long as a week to clear. Reporting live on the scene at Traveler's Junction, I'm Tammy Thatchmeyer, News Channel Ten."

After thanking Tammy, the News Ten anchor assured viewers they would be "standing by" for the latest breaking reports as the clean-up continued. He turned to the station's weathergirl to say, "Well Kim, at least our weather has stayed on track, with today's highs in the 80's as predicted…"

Ernie searched for where he had put the remote. He spotted Aformation sitting at the little desk where the motel left a thin, three-ring binder containing area restaurant menus and brochures advertising local activities. On the same desk was the yellow notebook. With an almost magic push of a button, the TV went silent.

"A train derailment! Who'd have guessed?" Ernie opened his lined ledger and flipped to a blank page. Thinking back on the day, he wrote down *Napoleon Hill*, the author of *Think and Grow Rich*. He would definitely re-read that book. If he remembered right, Hill was a journalist-turned-author who interviewed Andrew Carnegie and wound up writing the book as a sort of guide based on the philosophies of Carnegie and other titans of industry.

Ernie also remembered a story he had once heard on Paul Harvey's radio show about the same Andrew Carnegie who, as a teenager, worked as a night clerk at a railroad office. One late night he received a telegram from a panicked station operator saying a train had derailed and wrecked cars lay blocking the tracks — where they would remain for days until cargo could be transferred, etc. Carnegie studied the freight schedule and realized it would cost the railroad hundreds of thousands of dollars in lost revenue while the tracks were blocked. The teenager telegraphed back, *BURN THE CARS.* Not realizing the instructions were unauthorized and came from a kid, workers at the other end burned the cars, clearing the tracks in a matter of hours. So successful was the solution, the procedure became railroad policy— and Carnegie was promoted.

Apparently, Ernie thought, that doomed nineteenth-century train was not hauling diesel fuel. But Ernie also realized *Burn the Cars* could easily be the battle cry for 'clearing the tracks' of old mindsets, broken dreams, and bad habits. He decided he would remember the phrase whenever it became obvious he was stuck on something that didn't matter—or perhaps didn't matter as much as a better option.

F.O.R.D. Ernie wrote in his book, identifying the four factors Reverend Jackson said people hold most dear on the road of life. He stared at the acronym, thinking how everyone can identify with each factor, and how easy it is to take them for granted. He vowed he would become actively interested in other people's FORD, and with that vow understood that 'drive' has a double meaning. 'The Lord Drives a Ford' and some combination of their relationships with *Family, Occupation, Recreation, and Dreams* 'drives' most people.

And what was it the juggler had said? Oh, yeah, it's not about catching the balls, but releasing them. Ernie wrote down, *Make room for new ideas by letting go of old ones.* He followed that with (*Burn the Cars*) in parentheses.

He thought about the slovenly lady with the cigarette pampering the Acorn Queen, and hoped the young girl with the crown would not follow the same path as her elder. Flipping back a couple of pages in the yellow notebook, he re-read his notes on mastering his personal energy, and stopped on the line that read, "*I recognize that average is not acceptable, and will use the commonplace as a foundation to build uncommon results.*" It was an affirmation he did not have to pretend to believe, but he did need to practice it.

That night, Ernie tossed and turned, occasionally fighting with the noisy room air conditioner and more regularly with recurring indigestion. He had pleased Aformation by updating the yellow notebook, which was becoming part scheduler and part journal. He had made the most of the day's detours, and allowed himself to 'live in the moment' with each new experience. But there was still uneasiness, as if there were still unanswered questions about the day. Finally drifting off, Ernie's imagination launched another bizarre dream—this time without a cohesive story line. It was as if the synapses in his brain were misfiring.

Ernie—his feet nearly dragging the ground—was riding a tiny pony, which seemed to be unable to go in a straight line. The landscape was hazy, and nebulous objects came in an out of focus along their meandering path. First appearing in the haze was an enormous, 15-foot-tall Indian Chief, holding a huge corn dog up to his mouth, as if it was a cigar. The chief faded in the distance as Ernie and the pony plodded on down the road. Next, a large man in flowing purple and white robes passed them on a three-wheeled motorcycle trailing Japanese lanterns (like bouncing tin cans from a 'just married' car) and called out for Ernie to "Come join us for some popcorn!" Following him roared eight Harley-Davidsons ridden by elderly women, all smiling at him as they passed. From the haze, an ancient gothic hearse appeared. As it chugged slowly past them, Ernie saw Gomez and Mortisha waving from the front seat and Lurch standing on the back bumper as a footman. An unkempt woman wearing a tiara, cigarette angling from her mouth, was being filmed by a cameraman from the TV station as she made a halfhearted attempt to wave. Everyone in the dream seemed to notice Ernie, and they all seemed so friendly! The pony then passed by a thin blonde woman in sparkly blue eye shadow wearing a tuxedo and top hat, dancing with her cane to *I Shot the Sheriff.* Behind her was a smaller version of the same woman, a child, wearing an identical outfit and mimicking the woman's dance steps.

Ernie, still atop his pony as the haze turned into darkness, passed the scene of a train wreck, its crumpled yellow cars, looking very much like school busses, lighting up the night sky in a fiery blaze. Ernie followed the swirling cinders, glowing like sparks of pure energy, as they floated skyward and eventually drifted away from the wreck. They bobbed up and down in the unstable air and ultimately in and out of the hands of a short, bald juggler sitting atop a white tower several stories tall. He too, waved to the unlikely cowboy passing below. The pony transported Ernie beyond the fire and tower into the arched doorways of a great arena, and under stadium lights and a banner that read, ERNIE'S JOURNEY, Uncle Sam was pushing a lawnmower as he led a high school band playing *The National Emblem March.* Following the band was a Ford Mustang with a long-haired driver wearing a middle-eastern robe,   waving as if he knew everyone.

Cheers rose from an invisible crowd, and Ernie saw thousands of camera strobes flash like celestial fireworks.

As if all this was not strange enough, Ernie and the pony could see in the dim light ahead the six sisters from his imagined *Gone With the Wind* sequel—*Who, What, Where, When, How*, and the hand-wringing *Miss Why*, who was singly surrounded by a sympathetic A-Team. He couldn't quite make out what they were saying, but as he and the pony loped slowly past the cast, they stopped their conversation and glared at him, lips pursed.

Suddenly, the pony stopped walking. Standing in their path was an attractive woman with heavy makeup who had one finger in her ear and was looking directly at him, saying, "Reporting live from the road to Destiny City, I'm Tammy Thatchmeyer, News Channel Ten."

Ernie opened his eyes to discover it was still dark. "Connect the dots," Aha had advised. "Listen to the universe. Use that imagination of yours..." After his dream about Routine he had concluded that maybe his personal energy—his special gift—was his outrageous imagination, but after *this* dream, that idea seemed more like his special curse.

He stared at the dark ceiling and listened to the loud, constant hum of the air conditioner and just before falling back to sleep, again saw the six sisters in their corseted costumes come into view. This time, Scarlett O'Hara was among them, saying, "I can't think about that right now. If I do, I'll go crazy. I'll think about that tomorrow."

Attitude

On Guard

> People seem not to see that their opinion of the world
> is also a confession of character.
> **Ralph Waldo Emerson, "Worship,"**
> *The Conduct of Life*, **1860**

Tere was a knock at the door. Or at least it sounded like one above the din of the room AC. What in the world—who…?

Before Ernie could even get out of bed, it sounded again, but this time he wasn't sure it was a knock. It was more like muffled rifle shots—again and again. *Tump! Tump! Tump!*

Still sitting on the edge of his bed, he heard a second noise, more familiar. It was a circular saw. The tump-tumps continued. Someone was building something—just outside his window. Ernie peeked behind heavy drapes to discover daylight and three carpenters, one of whom was shooting a nail gun, constructing some kind of walkway or deck on the building next door to the motel. An air compressor kicked in, singing a duet with the air conditioner. The clock said 8:05.

No use lounging around anyway. Ernie hit the shower, which warmed his spirits and drowned the noise. He missed Glori. In fewer than 20 minutes he threw his things together, said good-bye to The Owl's Nest and was on a mission to find breakfast.

In the morning light, the community in which he had roosted for the night looked considerably more colorful and alive. Cars and trucks whizzed by him, and Ernie mingled with traffic for a few blocks toward the highway, his original route, before spotting a local restaurant called the Pruneville Pancake Palace. As he spun the Beetle into the parking lot, he noticed the palace guard by the front door—a full suit of dark purple metal armor standing at attention. When Ernie approached the entrance, he realized the tin man's lance had stabbed a stack of rubber pancakes. A sign identified him as *Sir Syrup*.

The A-Team was nowhere to be seen. Apparently, Ernie's mind was not yet fully awake. The Palace was busy, especially for a Monday morning. Heather, the hostess, seated him in a booth and handed him a plastic-covered menu. 'Heather'—wasn't that the name of Aunt B's hostess in his crazy robot dream?

"You're right, it was," whispered a brooding Awareness taking shape in the upholstered bench across from him, "which is kinda weird, considering there's a metal man just outside the door of this place."

"Man, that's creeping me out!" said the Dude, who was suddenly sitting beside him. "I hope this one doesn't chase you!"

"What would you like to drink?" a tall waiter in a stained apron asked Ernie.

"Coffee, black, thank you." He glanced at the menu. "And I'd like a short stack with bacon."

"Plain or buckwheat?"

"Oh, make it the wheat."

"Would you like your favorite syrup or a sampler?" Ernie must have looked confused, because the waiter continued. "It's a basket of eight of our most popular flavored syrups."

"Eight!? How many different flavors do you have?"

"We offer a total of 30, sir. You can see the list on the back of the menu."

"Wow! Yeah, bring me the sampler."

"You got it. I'll be back in a jiff."

Ernie flipped the menu over to see a photo of the sampler—a small wire crate with eight shot glass-sized containers of various color syrups—and below it a list of flavors. It started with Almond Maple and ended with Vanilla Cream. Among them were some that sounded tempting— Coconut Caramel ... Raspberry Rhubarb ... Orange Tango...

Ernie was reading all the names and trying to imagine the tastes, when he overheard a conversation at the table next to his. A man's voice was explaining to his companion something about the courts, and how judges assigned 'community service' penalties in lieu of jail time. It became apparent that the man talking was somehow in charge of finding appropriate 'volunteer' work, though the assignees were hardly volunteers.

"Some of these guys think they're too good to do clean-up jobs or work at a homeless shelter. And some of them even resist answering questions at the placement interview because they don't want to reveal their crime. Well, guess what? They were found guilty of something and I need to know *what* it was. I can't assign someone a job working with children if he's a pedophile."

The other person asked, "You mean they're embarrassed about their sentence? Sounds to me like they're getting off easy doing community service work."

"Well, of course they are! In fact, it's a shame it's considered punishment—my point is they think they're above it. Maybe it's a white-collar crime. You know, embezzling or something. They may not mind their friends knowing they are volunteering, in fact, they may even brag about that, but they don't want to get their hands dirty. Well, if the guy's crime is stealing from payroll, I can't allow him to work in a bookkeeping office."

The waiter brought a ceramic mug and a pitcher of coffee. As he poured the first cup and retrieved the menu, Ernie glanced over to see who was talking. It was a man with a neatly trimmed beard about his age in a necktie and sport coat, perhaps an attorney or non-profit director. The man with him was nicely dressed but wore no tie. Ernie wondered if, being so close to the highway, the two might be traveling to a meeting or conference out of town. Then he heard the waiter call him by name. "Would you like some more coffee, Mr. Justice?"

"Thank you, Junior, yes, I would." Mr. Justice waited for Junior to leave before continuing. "What really galls me is some of these self-important people would never volunteer for anything if they didn't have to. And often they're the very ones who criticize programs designed to help those in need. I mean, you can tell some have real disdain for any type of social program."

`His companion nodded. "My self-righteous brother-in-law sits in front of the TV watching those pseudo-news shows that mock the federal government. He has no clue about the problems in his own back yard. Does he lift a finger to help? Does he contribute to local charities? Of course not. His idea of 'giving back' is to write outrage letters to the editor echoing some half-truth he saw on TV."

Awereness leaned over and said, "Here comes our food."

Justice responded to his companion, "Well, that's not a crime, but it *is* a tragedy. I think most of those political cynics are looking to blame someone for their personal unhappiness, and it never occurs to them their attitude may actually foster their own underachievement. Unfortunately, it's a lot easier to sneer and complain than it is to get off your butt and do something productive."

Junior balanced a tray on the edge of Ernie's tabletop and transferred the plate with three pancakes and the eight-cylinder syrup basket. Ernie could feel steam rise from the fresh-off-the-griddle cakes and began reading the flavor labels, eager to choose one. He decided on Cinnamon Apple to start, and combined with a bite of pancake, it reminded him of hot apple pie. He was thinking about 'mom and apple pie' when, in concert with the bearded man's phrase *get off your butt and do something productive*, he thought of Trula Pickett. She had said something similar about people who *sit around on their fat be-hinds*. He thought back on that night at the theatre when she said, "It's never too late to make a contribution."

Ernie looked at the A-Team, who of course knew what he was thinking. He felt a little guilty and perhaps even a little ashamed. Though he had never written an angry letter to the editor arguing an ideological position, he was not exactly involved in his community, either—at least not outside his job at the theatre. He remembered his personal commitments to *no longer be a spectator, but a participant,* and to *positively impact the lives of others every day, even if in seemingly small ways.* Ernie suddenly realized that the key word was *positively*, because you could also impact others by being angry and bitter or sedentary and cynical.

The philosophers at the next table made their departure, and a busboy carrying a plastic tub quickly cleared their dishes. Ernie tried a total of six of the eight flavors before his short stack disappeared. His favorite, he decided, was Banana Walnut. He never tried the Prune Pecan.

"Thank you, Mr. Goforth," Heather read from his credit card. "Come back and see us!" The A-Team looked at the suit of armor suspiciously as they passed it on the way out. As they neared the Beetle, it looked to Ernie as if his car was leaning a bit.

"Oh, man, check this out," the wolf man said in a frustrated tone. Ernie looked down at the right front tire and it was nearly flat against the rim. He studied it a moment and remembered the construction project next to the Owl's Nest Motel. "Probably a nail," Awereness speculated.

Actionman encouraged Ernie to drive it to a repair place if he could find one nearby, rather than try changing the tire of a car sandwiched between others. The trick would be to find a shop nearby. Actionman's red cape billowed. "Back inside!" he ordered.

Once again they passed Sir Syrup, who now more than ever reminded Ernie of the robot Routine. And once again they met Heather.

"Oh, sure," she said. "Slick & Quick Auto Repair is just on the other side of the interstate. Stay on this road one, two—it's right past the third traffic light on the right."

Ernie backed up the Beetle slowly, careful not to turn the wheels too hard in the process, and drove slowly onto the road when the traffic thinned. So far, so good. Ernie heard a tick-tick-tick as the flat tire rotated against the pavement. They continued at a snail's pace, suffering a few glares and one impatient pick-up driver who yelled "Mo-ron!" But they arrived at Slick & Quick without incident, and parked parallel to the other cars lined abreast waiting their turn to occupy a repair bay.

The clerk, a big man with a shaved head and rings in each ear, asked, "What can I do for ya?" He barely looked up from the computer screen and continued entering some data before ceremoniously hitting *Enter* and finally giving Ernie his attention.

"I have a flat tire on that green Beetle, but I think it's just a nail."

"Need a plug," the big man said as if there was no doubt. Ernie decided he looked like Mr. Clean. "We're real busy at the moment. Monday mornin', ya know. But I'll try to squeeze you in after the next oil change." Ernie wondered if his shiny noggin represented the 'Slick' of Slick & Quick.

"Thanks," said Ernie, and he looked around for what to do in the meantime. Beyond a rack of tires and a display tree of fancy custom chrome wheels, Slick & Quick's idea of a reception area collected other trapped customers. Cheap plastic chairs formed the perimeter of an imagined room, the corners marked by careworn end tables stacked with old copies of *Car & Driver, Motor Trend,* and one stray issue of *Smithsonian.* A scowling man with his own spare tire hidden beneath his shirt sat staring at a TV, its screen filled with talking heads in a newsroom format. Awereness, visible to no one but Ernie, whispered "Hey, that's one of those shows the guy at the Pancake Palace was talking about."

Ernie had only seen bits and pieces of programs devoted to political commentary, and was surprised to hear the show personalities talking about the blockbuster movie *Safety Be Damned—in 3D.* 'This might help movie sales,' he thought. But it turned out the commentators were discussing how one-sided the movie had been, and how the producers had slanted the story against the real victim—the owners of the oil-drilling platform. Ernie watched in amazement as one important-sounding man actually began blaming the U.S. government for the disaster—an accusation Ernie knew had nothing to do with *the movie*. Besides—if the events in the fictionalized story were even close to what happened in real life—management shortcuts, explosions, fire, death, environmental damage, economic distress—the movie had captured the horror of the catastrophe, which was its goal. But before the discussion paused for an ad for *Working-Man Trucks*, the program's guest suggested the whole movie industry was part of a government conspiracy to blame the victim, cover up the truth, and profit by selling tickets to a naïve public.

"Go on—ask him!" encouraged Actionman. Ernie had for an instant thought about asking the scowling man watching this inventive report if he'd seen the movie. He had all but decided to avoid the subject when the man looked at him and began to speak.

"Those movie people are trying to ruin this country!" he snarled.

Ernie gave into his impulse. "Have you *seen* the movie?"

"They're not getting' *my* money," he declared.

Suddenly Attidude stepped in front of Ernie and said, "Stay cool, dude. Remember what Aha had you write down—the thing about mastering your personal energy."

In the same split second, Ernie saw Aformation look at his clipboard. The old soldier silently read him the whole passage: *I will master my personal energy by embracing excellence, ignoring negativity, and rejecting limitations.* This was chance to ignore some obvious negativity.

Almost simultaneously, Awereness stepped in. "It's more than a chance. You'll regret it if you argue with this poor man. You'll accomplish more good by staying positive."

Finally, Actionman said, "Offer him a free pass!"

With no discernable pause, Ernie responded to the negative man, "Well, let me know if you want to see it for free, and I'll pull some strings for you." And before giving the shocked man a business card, he wrote down his number. "This is my personal cell phone," he explained. "You can go to any Six Sisters Cinema that's showing the movie. Call me ahead of time and I'll make sure there's a pass waiting with your name on it."

"You don't *know* my name!" the man snarled, then stared. "You're one of *them*, aren't you?"

The wolf man growled. Attidude reminded him again to stay positive.

"I just thought if you haven't seen the movie they're discussing, you might like to—that's all." Ernie smiled. Others in the room had turned their attention away from the 'Summer Inventory Clearance Deals' at *Working-Man Trucks* to witness the conversation. The nasty man lifted his head to look down his nose at Ernie but said nothing. He then got up and walked toward the unisex restroom, the fleshy spare tire sagging over his belt.

"Wow," the Dude said. "How fun would it be to live with *him!?*" Ernie immediately thought of Glorianne, and how much 'fun' *he* must be first thing in the morning. Even the idea that such an attitude could impact a neutral mood made him cringe.

Mr. Clean appeared with a set of keys and said, "Mrs. Goodwin, we've got you fixed up."

An older lady with short, gray hair leaned over her plastic chair to grab her purse, and standing, leaned over again to say something to Ernie as she started for the counter. "I've seen the movie, and I thought it was amazing! That was a nice gesture you made." She stood upright, hoisted her purse strap over her shoulder, and added, "Oprah liked it, too."

Ernie smiled and nodded. The truth, known only to him, was that it was just a gesture. Six Sisters Cinemas had no policy or arrangement to exchange passes between theatres, and Ernie was only guessing he could make such an arrangement. It didn't matter, the scowling man was a victim of his own negativity—most likely of his own fears—and a sad example of missed opportunity.

A Different State

Things turn out best for the people who make the best out of the way things turn out.　　**Art Linkletter**

On the new generation of VW Beetles there is a small, clear plastic vial to the right of the steering wheel for use, the dealer had said, as a flower vase. Back when it was Glori's car, she had filled it with an artistic replica of a flower made from wire and colorful glass beads. It never needed watering, and never failed to amuse Ernie when he saw it. For him, it was a symbol of the girl he married—both whimsical and practical, simultaneously sophisticated and goofy. Today the beaded flower competed for trophy space with a bent nail. It was an apt souvenir, Ernie thought, of his morning spent in Pruneville.

After 24 hours of detours, delays, and deflated tires, it was good to be on the highway again. The A-Team was quiet, but Ernie knew from the Slick & Quick experience they would rally to assist him in real time—or even faster, if that's possible. While driving at a steady pace on all four properly inflated tires, he reminded himself of the four mission essentials each of his team represented—*attitude, awareness, affirmation, and action.* From there, he mentally went over the key points of mastering his personal energy—*embracing excellence, ignoring negativity, and rejecting limitations.* And perhaps most importantly, he repeated his vow to embrace a new level of confidence—*I recognize that average is not acceptable, and will use the commonplace as a foundation to build uncommon results."*

Ernie decided to use the time on the road to imagine how he might convert his "commonplace life" in Ordinary to a foundation for an uncommon future. He was imagining his daily routine when a Crown Victoria passed him—a *Ford.*

Family, Occupation, Recreation, and Dreams, he recited. Ernie began to picture himself interacting with his kids, and the image the woman with sparkly blue eye shadow working with her look-alike daughter flashed in his mind. He envisioned working with Willy and Karma at the theatre when he returned—a good start at becoming more involved in their lives. He would also find ways to strengthen his relationship with Glori. *Be aware of opportunities,* he thought.

In the *Occupation* category, he had created an actionable plan of sorts, and this trip proved he had initiated it. *I will no longer be a spectator, but a participant* .Ernie admitted to himself that his plan stopped short of having a specific goal, but interacting with the SSC senior management was new territory, and he had decided he shouldn't preclude failure, even if he wasn't sure what success might mean. *I will not decide in advance that I am bad at something,* he recited to justify his incomplete plan.

For Ernie, *Recreation* was even tougher. He enjoyed sports, but they were hardly a passion. He enjoyed family vacations, but they were few and far between. He enjoyed the movies, but movies were his occupation, weren't they? He began to imagine what activities brought him the most enjoyment. The only thing that came to mind was his interaction with other people, from the Lumberknots' dinner party to meetings with Aha to the conversation with the juggler. He enjoyed talking to Trula and the Iron Butterflies, and even enjoyed shop talk with Mrs. Broaderbuht. Ernie decided that deep down, he must be a 'people person.' Despite his inherent shyness, social interaction was his form of *Recreation*. No wonder the promise to connect with other people had struck a harmonic chord. He thought of the passage written in his yellow notebook: *I will endeavor to positively impact the lives of others every day, even if in seemingly small ways.*

Ernie was in an almost trancelike state, his subconscious—or non-conscious, to use a new-age term—was driving the car. Thank goodness Awereness noticed a sign for Newbeckon, 12 miles ahead. Somewhere in the recesses of Ernie's cluttered brain, he remembered that Six Sisters had recently announced plans to open a new multiplex in Newbeckon. Apparently, it was an architectural prototype for future theatre construction, and Ernie had wondered—even at the time he first learned of it—if the concession area would be different from that of his own theatre. Depending on how complete the construction was, this could be a chance to answer that question, as well as impress the management that he had already visited the new complex. He would take advantage of the *opportunity*.

Actionman stirred in the back seat. He was eager to get off his *be*-hind and do something constructive. Even the stoic Aformation looked forward to making some notes on the new construction to look over later. And Attidude was squirming. "I'm like, totally pumped!" he said, almost involuntarily.

A dozen miles later, Awereness pointed to the exit sign and mentioned to Ernie he should probably turn toward the most congested area, whichever that direction was, since none of them knew where this place was located. It turned out to be pretty simple. At the end of the exit ramp, Ernie could see a large open area with a chain link fence around it enclosing new construction and some heavy equipment, less than a block from the highway. He steered the Beetle toward it and parked in front of a large sign that read, *Coming Soon: Newbeckon Ridge—The Area's Best in Shopping, Dining, and Entertainment.*

Ernie searched for any hint of a ridge with no luck. Most of the new complex's façade was complete, but there were only a couple of locations with new signs affixed to it. There was, however, a building that appeared to be what he was looking for—a theatre. No Six Sisters Cinema marquee, yet— but telltale architectural features were in place:

ticket windows, a series of glass doors, and a brick arch that created the backdrop for the double S logo, designed to look like film threaded through a projector, with the tagalong letter C forming the profile of a lens. The construction gate, with its own sign that read AUTHORIZED PERSONNEL ONLY, was open.

Ernie drove in but parked a safe distance from a big truck with a telescopic boom that was apparently there to hoist some kind of sign—possibly the marquee itself—and made sure the business card he'd given the hostile man back in Pruneville was not the last one in his pocket. He then walked confidently up to the building, prepared to impersonate a Six Sisters executive if necessary, and entered the unfinished lobby without being questioned. What he saw was, well, disappointing.

"This looks just like your place," the wolf man announced. The Dude was frowning. Ernie noticed the gangplank to an arcade room, easily identified from the familiar counter and all the electrical outlets in the room. There was even an air-conditioning vent above the door.

"Let's check out the concession area," Ernie said hopefully.

"It might be bigger," said Awereness. "There looks like more cooler space, and there's a second countertop opposite the popcorn equipment," he reported.

The door to what would be the manager's office was missing, and Ernie glanced inside to discover that, unlike the concession area, the office was smaller. "Look," said Awereness, "there's no window into the hall. I guess they figure the manager needs to spend more time in the lobby."

Okay, there were some changes, but overall the space was divided up like every Six Sisters theatre he'd ever seen. It seemed to Ernie it was just more of the same. Was management stuck? Or did they think these microscopic alterations were revolutionary? Attidude noticed that their little tour was having a solemn effect on Ernie's hopeful expectations.

"I need to go to the bathroom," Actionman said, his cape billowing more than usual.

Outside, Ernie was walking back to his car when he noticed the truck's extended boom winching up an enormous sign that said in elegant, script letters, *Newbeckon Ridge*. He realized the sign, attached to a towering pole, was high enough to be seen by passing highway traffic. There was a man standing between Ernie and the truck, watching the installation with great interest through designer sunglasses.

"Pretty impressive, huh?" Ernie said authoritatively, hoping to disguise the fact he was trespassing.

"Yes it is," answered the man, who Ernie suddenly suspected of being in charge of the operation. "It's just within the range of our tallest truck boom—anything higher, and we'd have to bring in a serious crane."

"Are you with the sign company, then?" Ernie dared.

"No, I'm in the crane business," the man explained, still looking up. "Forgive the pun, but this job is beyond the reach of most sign companies."

Ernie stood beside the man, who was neatly dressed in casual clothes and sported a golf course tan. Together, they watched the assembly become perfectly vertical, then lift off the ground completely as a ground crew positioned the pole's horizontal flange over threaded rods rising from a concrete base. There were voice transmissions from the crew and crane operator coming from a radio holstered on the man's belt.

"Do they all go up like that?" Ernie asked.

"Like what? Oh, you mean in a single motion? No—only if you have the right equipment and a good erection team. The way we like to do it is have everything assembled and in place on the ground before it goes up. Are you with the builder?"

"Actually, no. I'm with the theatre. My name is Ernie Goforth."

"Pleased to meet you, Ernie. Excuse me a second." The man reached for the radio and asked simply, "We there?"

"We're there, boss."

The man smiled and extended his hand. My name is Deal—Isaac Deal. So you work with ol' Mo, huh?"

The only person Ernie had ever heard referred to as Mo—other than one third of the Three Stooges and one half of Mo-*ron*—was Morris Better. He realized he must be referring to the Six Sister's V.P. of Development. and wondered what connection Deal had with the man he was going to see. "You know Morris Better?"

"Oh yeah. I know him from the club. He's quite the character, isn't he?"

Ernie was not sure what this meant, but he played along. "Yeah, I don't talk to him often. We're in different cities and all, but I know he's sometimes hard to pin down."

"Well said. Mo is his own worst enemy—scurrying around, talking big—you never know what he's up to. And neither does he!" Deal laughed at his own humor. "So, you must live here in Newbeckon."

"No, I live in Ordinary. I'm actually headed to Destiny City to see... ol' Mo."

"You're kidding—that's where I live! So you mean to tell me we came from different directions and met hundreds of miles from home in a parking lot, and the thing we have in common is Mo Better? What a weird, small world we live in!"

Ernie said, "Well, it's not all coincidence, is it? I mean, we're both here because of this new shopping center, which has a Six Sisters multiplex..."

Deal stopped him. "This is the first time I've ever been on a construction site where your company is locating a theatre. We're from different states. We do entirely different things for a living. Yet in the first minute of our first conversation we discover we know the same guy. I'm telling you, it's a weird, small world."

Actionman appeared. "Invite him to lunch!"

"You want to grab a sandwich?" suggested Ernie.

"That's a great idea!" Deal responded. Let me talk to my crew for a moment, and I'll join you. But can we take my car? I'd rather not leave it here."

"Sure," Ernie said, and watched Deal walk toward the truck. He followed him just far enough to get a look at the name on the cab's door. It read, *IDEAL CRANE, Destiny City* followed by a phone number and website address.

"Good job, man," Awareness whispered. "This could be another opportunity."

"I wish he'd hurry up," Actionman said. "I really need to go to the bathroom."

Ernie thought he'd locked his car but decided to be sure. As he approached it, he saw a fiery red Porsche Carrera parked beside it with a vanity license plate that read IDEAL. 'I get it," he thought. 'Isaac Deal." Now he understood why he didn't want to leave his car. After a few moments, Ernie watched I. Deal swagger up to the driver's side of the Porsche smiling ear to ear. He had movie star good looks, with blonde streaks in his hair and a cleft chin. He looked a little like Kirk Douglas in his youth. In addition, his posture suggested supreme confidence.

"So, Ernie," I. Deal said as he throttled the high-performance machine out of the parking lot, "Tell me why you're going to Destiny City to see Mo Better."

Ernie hadn't thought about the *why* of it for some time. "I've been running the theatre in Ordinary for several years now and I see some opportunities to improve our profit margins—mostly through promotional events and enhanced concession sales. I'm meeting with 'Mo' to offer my ideas." Ernie noticed I. Deal did not enter the highway, but stayed on the local road.

"And what are you getting out of it?"

"Well, hopefully, a little credit—and maybe a chance to rise in the company."

I. Deal downshifted at a curve and accelerated out of it. Ernie was thankful he had his seat restraints buckled. "I hope you're pitching someone other than Mo while you're there!"

Ernie had the desire to explore that hope further, but felt uncomfortable quizzing his new friend so soon after they just met. Instead, he answered, "Oh, sure. Tell me, how did you get into the crane business?"

"Great question. Basically, I got tired of the sign business. That's why I made that remark about the project being out of reach for a sign company. I used to *own* a sign company, making the kind of signs grocery stores and gas stations use. So did three other people in Destiny City and we were all competing for the same customers. The sign business is hard enough without that—each job is a custom order, each is labor intensive, each requires design approvals and installation permits, blah, blah, blah. It's a mean business. One day I thought, what if I installed everybody *else's* signs? I'd take care of the trucks and they could contract the work to me. I'd even refer sign business to *them.*"

"So you bought the trucks?"

"No, I *leased* a truck boom—one big enough to handle most projects—kept one of my sign guys as a helper and started erecting other companies' signs. I made as much money in the first two months doing that as I did in the previous two years of building signs. I quickly discovered that, unlike a business that only makes signs, you can use a truck boom for a lot of things. Heck, we were helping take down dead trees, putting up roof trusses, all kinds of stuff—constantly. So I leased another truck. And another. In the meantime, I sold the sign company to one of my former competitors.

"Is that when you got a commercial crane?

"No, no—*heck* no. That's when I bought my first Porsche." I. Deal grinned and hit the gas. Ernie was pressed into the back of his seat from the acceleration. *"Feel the energy, Ernie!"* he could hear Aha saying.

Suddenly, I. Deal downshifted again and they pulled into *Bare Bones Barbecue.* "I found this place the last time I was in Newbeckon," Deal said. "If you don't like barbecue they have all kinds of sandwiches."

"I love barbecue!" Ernie answered. He knew this was a spot he'd never have found on his own, even with the A-Team in tow. "And I bet they have a bathroom!"

Ernie was surprised he had any appetite after eating pancakes with eight samples of syrup only hours before, but he had no problem finishing his sliced pork sandwich and onion rings. He listened to I. Deal explain how he loved to help other people solve their problems, whether that meant lowering an aging church steeple so it could be restored or lifting a palette of bricks for a mason three stories up. According to the man who was once tired of making signs, the crane business had been good to him. "Helping other people and making good money aren't mutually exclusive," he promised Ernie.

Before lunch was over Ernie learned I. Deal had three daughters, all of whom worshipped their father. The family lived in a stair-stepped house, once featured in Dream Home Digest, on the shore of the only lake of any size in Foundett County. In addition to German sports cars, he collected antique wooden boats, including two Chris Crafts and a Century. He was a member of the local country club, not because he liked golf, but because he liked being connected. His business sponsored charity events, and he volunteered his equipment and time to Habitat for Humanity. Despite his obvious affluence, there was nothing pretentious or arrogant about the man. He seemed genuinely appreciative of the people and things in his life.

"Hey! Let's get together when you're in Destiny City!" the movie star businessman suggested, still wearing his sunglasses. Ernie thought he actually saw his teeth sparkle.

"I'm only going to be there for a short time," Ernie said diplomatically. "But I really appreciate the offer."

"Well, you be sure to call me if you need anything. I know lots of people in town."

The trip back to the Newbeckon Ridge complex was just as harrowing as the sprint to *Bare Bones*, but the excitement Ernie felt was not all from the thrill ride. He pictured himself behind the wheel, driving to the lake house, overseeing a prosperous business... When I. Deal shut off the engine and they stepped into the quiet parking lot, Ernie couldn't resist one last question. "Tell me, Isaac, what motivates you? What's your *why*?"

"That's easy, friend. I enjoy it. I enjoy it *all*—helping people, making friends, building things—BIG things—and making a difference in my community. By the way, thanks for lunch—I owe you one." I. Deal grinned and gave a mock salute. Then he turned and headed toward the big shiny truck with its impressive boom still fully extended, reaching for the sky.

The Ogre

> If you are living out of a sense of obligation,
> you are a slave.   **Wayne Dyer**

After Newbeckon, the landscape soon became mile after mile of farmland. Corn, soybeans, pasture. Ernie drove for hours without seeing anything compelling enough to slow him down, or even interesting enough to inspire comments from Awereness, except of course, to remind Ernie to get gas. Sooner or later, it would be time to look for a promising place to stop for his final night on the road.

As the sun began to disappear behind a thick grove of pine trees in the distance, Ernie noticed an overpass and signs of civilization up ahead. There were gas stations, a couple of fast food places, and... yes, at least one motel. Ernie turned on his blinker.

At the end of the highway exit ramp was a city limit sign that read 'Responsibility.' Making sure there were no construction supplies in the parking lot, he parked the Beetle, grabbed his bag and checked into another modest motel, despite its dubious name, The Goodnight Inn. Ernie decided to take a shower before heading out to find dinner. That mission accomplished, he drove the Beetle, but as luck would have it, found a friendly-looking tavern with a noisy interior just a couple of blocks away, well within walking distance. *Chances R* looked like the perfect place to end the day,   and cruising through the lot, he noticed one space had a big green John Deere tractor parked in it. "That's pretty odd," the wolf man said.

Inside, he chose to sit in the bar area at a tall table with elevated chairs. Most of the noise, it turned out, was coming from competing TVs mounted on the walls, and only about half of the tables had patrons. At first he didn't notice the table next to his, or at least who was sitting there. Before the wait staff arrived, he caught a glimpse of an enormous individual.

Not usually one to stare, Ernie couldn't help himself. This man defined the word huge. Below his thick neck supporting at least two chins, a giant pair of overalls shrouded hundreds of pounds extending beyond the chair's seat. Ernie felt small.

A waitress appeared with a nametag that read Heather. 'Oh, no—not another Heather!' Ernie thought to himself. 'What's with all the Heathers!?'

"Hello, my name is Heather. I'll be your server this evening. What can I bring you to drink?"

With fatigue—and yes, somehow hunger—compromising his decorum, Ernie couldn't resist a sudden impulse to be silly. "I'll have what, uh, he's having" and discretely gestured toward his plus-sized neighbor.

Heather's multi-colored pigtails dangled back and forth as she leaned into Ernie and whispered, "Oh, no you *won't!* You have no idea what Obble's eating. His eatin' habits are *gross*."

"Hobble? Is that a name or a description?" Ernie asked Heather.

"No, it's Obble. AH-bul. His name is Obble LeGation. I think his family is from some other country."

"You're not serious. Really? I don't care if he's from another planet. What parents would name their child Obble?" By now Ernie was mostly talking to himself, but Heather answered anyway.

"Maybe in another language it means Bubba."

"Okay, maybe. And what does Obble gobble?"

Heather rolled her eyes and sighed dramatically. "Pretty much everything that's left over from the day before. He's been doing that every night since he found out the cook throws away food that isn't fresh. Obble says no one should let food go to waste."

"Instead, it's gone to waist," Ernie responded, proud of his pun, and gesturing to his own beltline.

Heather was not amused, but smiled anyway. "What can I bring you to drink?"

About that time Obble snorted audibly, and Ernie glanced over to witness him wiping his mouth with an enormous right arm, then licking his fat fingers. Ernie was reminded of his robot dream and Routine's polite but mechanical apology for eating with his fingers. "I'll have a Pepsi, please. And just bring me a nice dinner salad with blue cheese dressing."

An older gentleman, wearing red suspenders and carrying a straw hat, passed by Ernie's table and nodded to the heavy man, "Hello there, Ob! How are things at home?"

Obble again wiped his mouth on his arm, and replied in a voice that reminded Ernie of a fog horn with sinus problems. "Oh, hello Mr. Oliver. Mother is doing very well, thank you. I've just slipped out for a little late snack." He then added, as if to assure the kind man he hadn't forgotten his mom, "I ate with Mother at home."

Mr. Oliver paused at Obble's table but remained standing. "You know, Ob, you really don't have to eat every meal with your mother. I'm sure she expects her grown son to have a life of his own. Maybe you could go on a fishing trip or even go bowling once in a while."

"Oh no, Mr. Oliver. I could never do that. I promised Mother I would always be there to take care of her. I feel guilty just being here at Chances. But tonight we did play Scrabble."

A mental picture of Obble picking up little wooden Scrabble tiles formed in Ernie's mind. 'I'll bet he's all thumbs," he joked to himself, still in his silly mood.

Mr. Oliver smiled and idly turned the brim of his hat in a circular motion with his wrinkled hands. "Well, Ob, tell your mother I said 'Hello' and promise me you'll think about branching out a little. I'm sure your mother would like that."

"I'll do that," Obble bellowed. "And please tell Mrs. Oliver I said hello."

Heather patiently waited until Mr. Oliver strolled past her before delivering the salad to Ernie's table. He heard a low rumble and hoped Obble had simply suppressed a burp. "Can I get you anything else?" Heather said, her rainbow pigtails draped over her shoulders.

"No thanks, this looks good," Ernie answered. "But you may be able to answer a question..." He lowered his voice. "How long have you known Obble?"

"Oh, pretty much all my life," smiled Heather. She repositioned herself so that her back interrupted Obble's line of sight, and began whispering. "He looks scary, but he's harmless enough—at least most of the time. He just works on his parents' farm. Well, his mama's farm now...his daddy died about five or six years ago. He is unbelievably strong."

"I assume his father was a big man, too?"

"Oh, not really. I mean, he was just average. And his mama is a tiny little thing. I think maybe he's gotten so big 'cause he carries around such a heavy burden. I mean, takin' care of the farm all by hisself and his mama and all. It's kinda sad, ain't it?" She glanced up at the tavern's bar framed in neon advertising. "I gotta get back now."

Heather pivoted to make her exit, lifting her pigtails into a low orbit. Ernie began crunching on cucumber and croutons, at one point looking up to see Obble staring at him. Even his gaze seemed to have weight. When their eyes accidently met, Ernie ventured an attempt at conversation. "Hi. About how far is Destiny City from here?"

Looking directly at Obble, Ernie studied him more closely. His head hosted only a wisp of hair, but his eyebrows looked like huge caterpillars. His expression—part anger, part resignation—seemed permanently sculpted on his face. Ernie had the sense that inside this ogre of a body was deep sadness, just as Heather had speculated.

Obble raised an enormous arm from its resting elbow and held up the sky with his palm. "Why do you have to go to Destiny City? It's quite a distance."

Ernie smiled and answered, "Well, no one is *making* me go there, but I still want to." He hoped the response didn't sound patronizing. He also did not want to begin a lengthy conversation about his line of work, or as I. Deal might have said, 'blah, blah, blah.'

The big man's eyes looked perplexed. "You mean you have no real reason to go—you just want to?" Ernie noticed he wasn't smiling.

"I suppose you could say that—but 'wanting to' might be enough of a reason, don't you think?" Ernie naively expected Obble to agree with him, in the spirit of light conversation. He was wrong.

"I think a man should do right by his commitments. I'll bet you're running away from something, aren't you?" Obble's caterpillars arched with suspicion.

Ernie had not expected such an innocent question to become an instant challenge. Perhaps Obble had heard Heather talking about him—not behind his back, but from behind hers. Or perhaps Ernie had stumbled onto a painful subject for the big man. He remembered Glorianne once observing that a person's response is not always to what you say—but to what that person hears. "Well, the only thing I could be accused of running away from is a dull routine. I believe Destiny City may hold the key to a better life for me."

Awereness whispered in Ernie's ear, "I'm pretty sure that was not the smartest thing you could have said."

Obble stared, chewing the residue of whatever had been in his last bite of leftovers. Several seconds passed before his thoughts turned into words. "The grass is always greener!" he roared accusingly, and allowed his massive arm to fall on the table, shaking the pitcher he was using as a glass. "You don't like what's expected of you, so you're running away to greener pastures."

What an extraordinary response! How could well-intentioned conversation go so wrong? "I certainly did not mean to offend you," Ernie said to mitigate the misunderstanding. "I fully plan to return home once I have some answers."

Ernie had realized too late the big man had a black or white, right or wrong way of looking at things. His self-imposed limitations were founded in a naïve understanding of faith, family, and fortitude. In Obble's mind, the person who would abandon what he was taught— or even his chores—in order to chase some selfish idea of a better life was weak-willed and promiscuous. Ernie was a stranger in his constrained world, and represented a perverse sense of entitlement that was, in Obble's rationale, despicable.

"I don't really know or care what you *plan* to do," Obble rumbled, "but I think you believe you are better than us."

Suddenly, Ernie realized that the big man had slotted him into a "we *vs.* they" category, a giant leap of conclusion for such a small question of geography. It was as if this ogre was looking for a confrontation and Ernie had inadvertently provided one. "Mr., I have no such belief. I truly am sorry, I was just asking if you happen to know how far it is to Destiny City. My mistake, really."

As Obble began to stand up, a layer of his massive stomach caught the edge of the table, pitching it forward. Though no food remained, there were bowls and platters and serving utensils that slid and tumbled onto the floor with such a crash that the whole place became instantly quiet, except for the voices of sportscasters on the TVs. For the first time that evening, Ernie felt certain fear when Obble looked at him—as if he were somehow the cause of this catastrophe.

Heather threaded her way through the tavern, and discovering Obble glaring at Ernie, said, "You didn't say nothin' about his mama, did you?"

"Mother! What did you say about *Mother!?*" thundered the giant, and Ernie's mouth went dry. It didn't matter; in that instant he forgot how to talk anyway. He may as well have been looking into the face of a mother lion defending her cubs, except this was the cub defending his mama. Ernie's only thought was escape, and he realized the exit was on the far side of Obble and the turned-over table.

Suddenly Mr. Oliver appeared. "Ob, son, please don't get excited. I'm sure this man had no intention of upsetting you. Now, if you will just..." Obble's stare left Ernie for just a second to face Mr. Oliver, and it was in that second that Ernie saw Actionman.

"Dive for the door!" the caped muse ordered. Ernie scrambled off his chair and hurled himself over the scattered dishes along the floor with the intention of slipping past the angry beast, but slipped on the wet floor instead.

His attention to Mr. Oliver broken by the clamor, Obble rotated his enormous frame to snag the insolent outsider, but he was nowhere to be seen. Terrified, Ernie realized that his stumble had placed him directly under the overhang of the monster's enormous belly.

Obble continued to rotate, searching for his enemy. Frozen, Ernie watched as the ogre faced the door, and stood up when Obble's back was completely turned. Hiding behind him, Ernie moved in harmony with Obble's Doppler rotation, staying just out of sight. Mr. Oliver, Heather, and the others watched this uncanny dance, but no one took sides or gave away Ernie's location. By the time Obble figured out where Ernie was, it was too late and the man seeking Destiny City continued his pilgrimage in a sprint—his invisible A-Team trailing behind him.

Out the door and nearly to the Beetle, Ernie heard the fog horn bellow through the dimly lit sea of cars. "You cowardly, little man! You can't insult Responsibility and get away with it! Stop running away! Remember you're no better than anyone else!"

Safe in his car, Ernie drove the Beetle as if it were I. Deal's Porsche, peeling out of the Chances R parking lot, swerving off the service road and onto the highway. The Dude was screaming, "Go! Go! Go!" Ernie was six miles down the road before he calmed down enough to remember his clothes and toiletries were back at the motel.

Awereness was considerably calmer than Attidude. "At this speed, he'll have a hard time catching you with his big green tractor." Ernie realized what the wolf man was trying to tell him, took his foot off the gas, and turned around at the next exit.

While sneaking back into town, Aformation suggested Ernie write in his yellow notebook, "You can't hide behind Ob LeGation."

Awareness

That's not a wink

> I spent my whole life not knowing what I want out of
> it, just chasing my tail. Now for the first time I know
> exactly what I want and who... that's the damnable
> misery of it.   **Curt Russell as Wyatt Earp**
> **in the 1993 movie *Tombstone***

Ernie poured coffee into a foam cup and asked the Goodnight Inn's morning desk clerk, "Do you ever go to Chances R?"

"Yeah, sometimes," the plucky young woman behind the counter said, smiling. "Are you asking me out?"

Even though he knew she was teasing, he felt himself blushing. "No, I need a big favor. When they open, will you take this envelope to Heather?"

"Oh," the clerk said, rolling her eyes. "I see what you're doing! We haven't even been on our first date yet and you're already two-timing me!" She grinned at her own wit. "I'll be happy to."

Ernie thanked her and grabbed his bag to duck out of Responsibility. In less than two minutes he was on the highway, settling into traffic. Destiny City was still about four hours away.

Tired from a fitful sleep, he drove conservatively in the right lane, not wanting to be bothered with the temptation to cheat the speed limit. Staring at the nearly empty road ahead, he caught glimpses of last night's dream following the incident with Obble, though this one was not nearly as vivid as those about a robot giving chase or characters in a parade. It was more of a slide show, or random visions of this and that. Not surprisingly, many of the images were of a huge man in overalls, riding a tractor in a dusty field plowing an endless sea of furrows, the relentless growl of the engine accompanying the tedium. Ernie could see Obble's great bulk balanced on the machine, his formidable hands grasping the wheel with resolve to stay the course, to ride out his responsibilities. It was all a matter of perception, of course. Ernie felt obligations too, like the one to pay for his meal from the night before. That's why he left an envelope for Heather.

"You know," Awareness said, looking straight ahead. "That big, green tractor he drives says a lot about who he is and what choices he's made in life. It's like the cars on this road. You can often deduce a driver's personality just by the car he or she is driving."

"Not always. Look what I'm driving," Ernie replied.

"True. But look what you're *not* driving. You are not driving a bright red Porsche. You are not driving a black and pink Harley-Davidson. You are not driving a big green John Deere."

Ernie pictured the obese man driving his tractor as a *choice*. He remembered what Heather had said. "I think maybe he's gotten so big because he carries around such a heavy burden." Lots of people carry a heavy burden, he thought. Lots of people have weighty obligations. They don't necessarily outgrow all their clothes.

"The big man sees no way out, though." Awereness said, even though Ernie had not voiced his thoughts out loud. "He doesn't have a wife or kids or the possibility ˙of promotion. He's stuck in Responsibility."

Ernie began thinking about other people who felt like they were at a dead end, obligated by family expectations or self-image. Part of that feeling may be limited exposure to opportunity, or inability to accept different ways of thinking. Ernie even had the feeling that Aha may have seen some of those same limitations in him, although in his case they would be almost surely self-imposed.

He eased off the gas as he approached a slower car in his lane. The A-Team watched out the window as they moved into the passing lane and overtook a battered pick-up truck challenging its suspension with a heaping load of watermelons. The truck's driver looked straight ahead, the story of his workaday life etched on his weathered face.

"He's doin' the best he can," narrated Attidude.

Examining the truck as he passed, Ernie returned to the thought of what he was *not* driving. He didn't completely embrace the idea that cars match the personalities of their owners, the way some say people look like their dogs. But he didn't drive I. Deal's Porsche or even Aha's BMW because he couldn't afford it, but rather because he had different priorities. Suddenly Ernie realized that, even if there was no *why*, there was in fact a *why NOT* reason he didn't spend so much money on an expensive vehicle. There were more important things to spend that money on than sports cars or luxury sedans.

"So, what are they? Where do you spend your hard-earned money?" the wolf man wanted to know.

"Well, the house, cars, food, insurance, the usual things…"

"So you place a high value on the 'usual things' that a good family provider strives for."

"Of course!" Ernie replied to his imaginary antagonist.

"So more than anything, your *why* is supporting your family. Right?"

"The main thing—sure."

Awereness was relentless. "But you could go work somewhere in a foreign country and just send money to your family if paying the bills was all there was to it. I think you're saying 'family' is your *why* because it's the noble and correct thing for a father to say, and you want to be a good dad. And you want to be *thought of* as a good dad. That is so typical—so *average*."

Ernie was confused. He *did* want to be a good dad and a good husband. But just making money to support the family was not the definition of a good family man. He wanted to be a part of their lives as well. *A participant, not a spectator.* And he knew that Awareness was also reminding him of his ability to channel his personal energy, and *recognize that average is not acceptable.*

Quiet for miles, suddenly Aformation joined in the thought conversation. "It's good you're referring to those notebook passages, but there's one you never bothered to write down. Remember when I. Deal said 'helping others and making good money are not mutually exclusive?' Well, that same principle might apply to being a good dad. I don't think you have to be a martyr to be a responsible spouse or parent. It's like Obble. You don't have to stay at home and play Scrabble with your mother every night to be a good son."

Ernie watched the broken white lines of the highway click by. He considered how he had occasionally used the responsibilities of fatherhood as an excuse for underachievement, or as Aformation had put it, "hiding behind obligation." Was he planning to wait until both Karma and Willy were out of school and away from home before taking a career risk? Was this trip to headquarters and his timid presentation a lukewarm attempt to simply confirm his status as a good company soldier?

Tinny music came from the cup holder. His phone was singing, 'Tell me something good.'

He glanced at the number. It was Glorianne. "Hi, Babe! How's life in the jungle?"

For the next several minutes, Glorianne excitedly told him about her adventure thus far; stories of the plane trip and delayed luggage, a description of the retreat facility—a series of huts with mosquito nets over the beds. She described the dining room hostess who had native dark skin but bright blue eyes, the meandering pathways and lush gardens. She went on to describe the Cosmic Encounters activities, which included discussion groups, lectures, hikes, games, and meditation exercises. She talked about meeting a new best friend named Constance, seeing an amazing tree house, and trying something called a zip line. Ernie sat and listened, genuinely interested. And how was *his* trip going, she wanted to know.

"Great so far," Ernie said. He told her of a few setbacks, casually mentioning a detour and the flat tire. But those things were minor nuisances, he assured her, and he would be in Destiny City in a few hours now. He silently decided that tales of parade jugglers, wild car rides, and ogre confrontations would be better told another time. "I love you, Glori."

"Aw, honey, that's sweet. I love you, too. I'll call you in a couple of days, OK?"

"Have you talked to the kids?"

"No, but why don't you call them, and tell them we've chatted."

"Will do. Make sure that zip line is buckled up tight. We wouldn't want to lose you!"

After hanging up, Ernie pictured Glorianne high above the jungle canopy on a platform, her harness attached to a pulley dangling from a long cable stretched to the next tower. She would have to find the courage to let go in order to 'zip' to the other side, suspended in mid air. He thought about the juggler's lesson that his craft was not about the catch, but about the release. For Glori to make it across the abyss, she would have to let go.

From there, Ernie thought about Obble's inability to let go of his distorted perception of responsibility. He thought about the need some people have to reprogram their robotic Routine. Maybe this applied to him, too. He remembered I. Deal's story of how he let go of building signs in order to build a new business. Ernie finally concluded that in order to achieve a new level of success, he had to let go of his old ways of thinking.

"So," Awareness summarized. "You know you need to release some of those tired old ideas before you can catch some new ones— ideas that are floating around the universe. You understand that it's a forgone conclusion a well-planned mission will succeed once you've employed the four key elements. The only thing you don't know is *why* you might want to achieve a new level of success. Is that about it?"

Ernie said, "Yeah, that's pretty much it."

Awereness, in the coarse whisper that almost dared you to listen, challenged him. "But you do. You already know your *why*. It's just not so glamorous."

Ernie no longer noticed the cars around him. The Beetle became the big green tractor plowing an endless asphalt field. His non-conscious was now driving, and he realized he was traveling to Destiny City at expressway speeds on a mission that—if successful—could well cement his ties to the job he now questioned. "Why is this trip a good idea?" he asked out loud.

"What you really want to know is *why not*," came the answer in a whisper.

What did he think would happen? If they adopted his ideas, what would be his reward? A small raise? Time on the road? A thank you? Those reasons certainly weren't why he was charging ahead.

"You already know your *why*," Awereness repeated.

Ernie snapped back into the real world when Awereness noticed a large sign placed in a roadside meadow that read 'TOMBSTONE SALOON, Breakfast-Lunch-Dinner.' "Want to stop for some breakfast?" the werewolf asked.

"Yes!" said Actionman before Ernie could even process the question. *Tombstone* was one of Ernie's favorite movies. He pictured a raucous place with swinging saloon doors and a player piano clanking out *Camptown Races*—perhaps ladies in hoop skirts would be servers. Ernie and the A-Team took the next exit.

At the end of the exit ramp, Ernie searched for a sign of the saloon, but saw only fast food franchises with drive-through windows. Awareness suggested they explore the direction away from the congestion. About a quarter mile from the intersection, they saw it— the Tombstone Saloon—a quaint, rustic building with a hitching post out front. But along its weed-infested parking area, a dusty sign announced it was CLOSED.

"Wow, it's true to its name!" Attidude said. "Pretty dead."

Ernie said, "I've got an idea," and turned the Beetle around in the dry, unpaved entrance, leaving a cloud of dust. "Let's go get an egg biscuit and come back."

After a few minutes, the A-Team returned to Tombstone with a fresh cup of coffee and breakfast in a bag. The parking lot was surrounded by a split-rail fence, giving it the appearance of a corral. Ernie decided that the place would make a great movie set and when he stepped up on a wooden 'rocking chair porch,' he spied what was left of an old ladder-back chair, its cane seat torn away. There he sat awkwardly, propping his feat on the railing. Most of the traffic coming off the highway was headed in the other direction—perhaps one of the reasons the Tombstone Saloon had tumbleweeds.

He ate the greasy biscuit slowly, hoping the coffee would cool enough to drink before the food got too cold to eat. "I've decided I'm going to listen to the universe," Ernie announced to his clan. He had no experience in the practice of meditation, but this seemed like a nice quiet place to make a deliberate effort to 'plug in' without the distractions of people or gadgets. After some critical insights were realized just that morning, he felt he might be close to finally answering the *why* question plaguing him for weeks, and this surreal setting seemed uncommonly distant from Ordinary.

He turned off his cell phone and sat quietly with his eyes closed, trying to neutralize any modern-day noises. He felt a slight breeze, and discovered other sounds he hadn't heard at first—some kind of crickets chirping, random birds singing, the creaking of his wobbly chair. He sat still and tried to turn off that exhausting imagination of his, dismissing the A-Team muses from their duties, and instead focusing on the simple patterns of his day-to-day life—getting up in the morning, eating breakfast, running errands, going to work. Eating popcorn. Coming home from work, days off from work. Seeing the kids. Chores. The patterns repeated like the endless plowed furrows.

As he sifted through the mental images to capture a sense of who Ernest Lee Goforth was, or perhaps who he had become, a vision of that late night scene and its fatal accident flashed onto his mental movie screen. There against a confusing backdrop of darkness and a swinging traffic light was the shadowy figure with a flashlight approaching the crumpled Camaro, a policeman waving off others, gesturing for would-be helpers to keep their distance, followed by the quick blue-white spark of electricity that ended the Samaritan's life. Ernie could only imagine what the policeman's personal legacy was. He left a wife and small child—that much was known from the newspaper. But what had he accomplished before his life was tragically interrupted?

That's it. That's *IT!* Never mind what the policeman had accomplished, what had *Ernie Goforth* accomplished—really? 'The usual things' would not qualify in this case... *average is not acceptable*, he thought. He wanted something better than average, and if honest with himself, he had *always* wanted something beyond average. He wanted it long before Aha had coached him on mastery. He desired prosperity...recognition—he wanted to make a difference in people's lives. Ernie's *why* was not earth shattering—it was earth *improving.* He simply wanted his life to be a positive influence on the world around him—to help others, to support and influence his kids *and others*, to make a real difference—a real contribution. Being a good dad was only a part of that. Besides, if he made a positive influence on the world around him, his family would naturally be at the center of it all.

And, as if fast forwarding a problem-solving sequence, he decided he would do this by channeling his energy and focusing it on productive and rewarding endeavors, even simple ones, always making sure his *why* was part of the plan. It was really as simple as that, and not so far from the affirmations he was already writing down. His *why and how* had arrived from the universe and entered Tombstone as a twosome, as if Wyatt Earp and Doc Holiday had rode into town together.

"Hey Ernie, the sheriff's in town." Awereness said.

"Yep, I know, but please don't bother me now."

"Well, I think you better wake up because he might bother *you.*"

Ernie reluctantly opened his eyes and saw a man in a uniform walking toward him. Then he noticed the squad car parked in the dirt lot beside the Beetle. The law had arrived in a car marked Sheriff—but it was not Wyatt Earp.

"Good morning," the officer said politely. "Taking a nap?" The uniformed man was unusually tall, and though he was smiling, projected a look of suspicion. He wore neither hat nor sunglasses, despite his nearly white complexion and orange hair. He did, however, squint against the glare of the morning sun.

"Just stopping to eat a bite of breakfast. Seems like a quiet place to have a cup of coffee."

The deputy's smile turned into a grimace. "Well," he said, "I guess it is. But there's a problem because this quiet place is private property, and my guess is, it's not *your* private property."

Ernie sprang to his feet. "I'm sorry. I didn't think of my sitting here as a form of trespassing, but I suppose it looks that way."

"It looks that way. But if you're planning to move along, I don't suppose there's any harm done." He paused and seemed to wink. "You are planning to move along, right?" The deputy winked again—twice.

"Oh, yes sir. I'm finished anyway." Ernie crumpled his empty bag and picked up the nearly finished coffee cup. He noticed yet another wink, and suddenly Awereness whispered in his ear: *That's no wink, that's a tic—an involuntary blink. Don't fool around with this guy.*

"I really didn't think of it as trespassing, I just stopped for a break."

"I appreciate your cooperation. You have a good trip." The officer 'winked' twice more and walked back to his car, but stood by the door calling in on his radio. Ernie started the Beetle and drove slowly out of the Tombstone's corral, heading toward the highway.

Ernie could not resist looking in his mirror to make sure the winking deputy wasn't following him, but there was no 'county mountie' in the reflection.

"I think that tall man really likes you," Attidude said. Ernie glared at the Dude with mild disgust.

He's on a mission

That is why, no matter how desperate the predicament is, I am always very much in earnest about clutching my cane, straightening my derby hat and fixing my tie, even though I have just landed on my head.

Charlie Chaplin

"Well, look at the new Ernie," Awereness said in his Al Pacino dryness. It was easy to tell he was being sarcastic. "He figures out he wants to be above average and nearly gets arrested at the same time! Yes, sir. Ernie, the *make-a positive-impact* guy, whose only impact so far is trespassing on someone's property."

Attidude puffed up. "Ernie was minding his own business—in fact, trying to improve himself, and wasn't hurting anyone. He just chose an awkward place to contemplate."

"Awkward. Yeah, that's Ernie Goforth. *Ernie the loser.*" Ernie glanced over to his alter ego and noticed the wolf man's eyes looking wild and distant. Both his nose and facial hair seemed to be longer than before.

The Dude defended him. "Hey, it was just a misunderstanding. It could happen to anyone, or at least, to anyone trying to accomplish something. Nothing ventured, nothing gained. Brush it off, man. It's not worth worrying about."

The Beetle was quiet for several miles. Awereness finally broke the silence with his more familiar whisper. "It's kind of funny, really."

"Yes, but I think there's something to be realized here." The voice was Aformation's, who saw the episode as a learning experience. "It's really not enough to say you're going to be this or that, or just announcing the intent to become better at something. You have to actually become the image of the person you aspire to be. Start being that person immediately, not somewhere down the road."

Attidude responded, "Oh come on, give the man a chance!" He's barely figured out *why*, and you're saying do it now! Do *what* now?"

Awereness chimed in. "Ernie's discovered only half of his why—the part that has to do with conviction. He now understands that he wants to be above average, or do more than just get by in life. He still has to find the other half of it—the part that has to do with passion."

"They're not the same thing?" the Dude asked.

"Not necessarily. Let's say your *conviction*, or firm belief, is that you are put on this earth to help people with disabilities. Your *passion* might be providing wheel chairs for disabled children. In Ernie's case, his *conviction* might be that, for him, average is not acceptable—but he's decided his *passion* is to positively impact the lives of others. How does he do that? What is it that Ernie can do to make that happen? He still has to figure that out." Awereness sat back and crossed his arms, as if resting his case.

Attidude said, "Seems to me you're describing *how* and *what*. I want to be upbeat about this, but I'm confused.

The werewolf frowned. "In the disability example, *Who* would be you and/or the disabled kids. *What* would be the wheelchairs. *How* is more like a business plan—finding a way to get the money to buy the wheelchairs. None of those represent *why*. *Why* is the motivation to make it happen. That motivation consists of both conviction and passion." Surely this will settle it, Awereness concluded.

Ernie continued to drive, listening closely to his A-Team debate the meaning of *why*. The image of the six sisters flashed through his mind—*Who, What, Where, When, How*—standing out in the garden in their bustles and bonnets discussing their anxious sister *Why*. Now they were saying she had a split personality?

Aformation cleared his throat. "This is why we write things down—to form a clear understanding of the mission. Earlier, I said Ernie should start behaving as the man he wants to be *immediately*. I don't disagree that you have to be motivated, or that commitment is a complement to passion. They're two sides of the same coin. But you don't have to know all the details before you start becoming the person you want to be. That's why we keep writing down these principles and ideas. Ernie doesn't have to know his ultimate passion before he begins making a positive impact on others. All those things—*mastering personal energy, being aware of opportunities, connecting the dots*—must represent what he already does, not what he wants to do."

Suddenly, Ernie again remembered what Yoda said in *Star Wars*, "Do or do not. There is no try."

For a superhero, Actionman had been largely worthless on the road. His influence was generally limited to decisions involving the stomach—either feeding it or emptying it. Philosophy was the domain of his teammates. Thus it was a big surprise when he suddenly entered the conversation. "It's time we converted those affirmations into action," he said, agreeing with the soldier's assessment. "From now on, Ernie will no longer say, *I will master my personal energy*, but rather, *I channel my personal energy to make a positive impact*."

"Wow, that's very good!" Attidude acknowledged.

"Thanks. It's my area," Actionman boasted.

Sure enough, Ernie realized, at some point an affirmation becomes an action. It makes no sense to keep repeating over and over that you *will* do something once you can actually do it. Perhaps tonight he would review and revise his yellow notebook.

"No," said Actionman. "Tonight we *will* revise the notebook— not perhaps." His red cape was billowing. Teammates looked at each other, sharing the satisfaction that something would come of their collective efforts.

"I just want to add one thing..." said Awereness. "All this talk about finding Ernie's passion might suggest there's a single endeavor or special focus he's looking for. But Ernie's a complex guy. He has lots of interests, multiple relationships, and different aspirations. He might have several things that qualify as passions, and no one focus could satisfy them all. I think that's where Attidude plays a major role—to remind our guy that his *why* need not be one dimensional."

Ernie glanced in the mirror to see the Dude beaming. The muse looked somehow more dignified, perhaps more confident. Ernie understood what the wolf man was saying, but he also knew that without a primary passion, it would be hard to channel his personal energy into a unified success. There was still work to be done. *Connect the dots,* Aha had advised.

Taking his foot off the gas pedal, Ernie checked the side mirror to see if anyone was passing him before he pulled into the left lane. There was another slow vehicle in the right lane, this time... no wait, it was the *same* vehicle as last time. Apparently the old battered truck weighted down with watermelons had passed them while they were at the Tombstone Saloon, and now they had caught up with it again. The driver continued to look straight ahead.

"He's on a mission." Awereness deduced. "And I just believe he'll succeed."

Aformation added, "It has never even occurred to him he could fail."

No sooner had they passed the old truck a second time than Awereness pointed to a sign reading REST STOP. "Do you realize how long it's been since you drank that second cup of coffee?" he asked. Ernie turned on his blinker.

"Hey, when we stop you should give the kids a call," Attidude suggested.

"First things first," pleaded Actionman. Ernie parked the Beetle and everyone spilled out onto the hot pavement. There were several cars in the parking lot, but none directly beside the Beetle... at least as they entered the building housing restrooms. While inside, Ernie studied a roadmap locked behind a Plexiglas cover that posted an arrow with the words, "You Are Here."

"Check it out, man! Destiny City is just over there," Attidude said, pointing. Ernie watched him trace his finger along the double line representing the highway route they were traveling. There was a large lake they would cross over before reaching the city limits—'probably where I. Deal lives,' he thought.

Rested, the Team headed back to the Beetle, and Ernie thought he would sit there and make the phone calls to Karma and Willy before they left again. But as they approached the parking lot, Ernie heard loud music coming from a dark purple car now parked beside his. The car was an 80's era Ford sedan, modified to sit as low as possible. With windows down and volume up, the stereo serenaded the parking lot—and the highway beyond—with a pulsing base that seemed to vibrate Ernie's teeth. He wasn't sure whether this was the genre known as rap or hip hop, but he was sure it was too loud. It was as if the car was screaming "look at me!"

Ernie then noticed a huge orange Ford pick-up truck, the body—decorated with NASCAR and NRA decals—was raised high above the wheels and chassis. It had enormous tires and huge chrome pipes that vibrated as it rumbled into the parking lot. The driver revved the engine, and it occurred to Ernie there must be pieces missing from the muffler. The truck seemed to be screaming, "look at me!"

The contrast between the two vehicles could not have been sharper, yet each had key things in common. Both had been radically modified from their factory design. Both were attempts to make a statement—no doubt a similar statement—to different American cultures. More than anything else, it struck Ernie that each sported the letters F.O.R.D. If those letters could be considered to represent Family, Occupation, Recreation, and Dreams, the drivers of both vehicles surely had those in common as well.

Amazingly, the obnoxious truck parked on the other side of the Beetle, and Ernie saw that his little green car looked strange sandwiched between the two competing egos. For a fleeting moment he thought the pledge to make an impact on anyone, let alone everyone, was a really bad idea. And then he remembered the very first affirmation he ever wrote: *I will not decide in advance that I am bad at something.*

Ernie opened the door to his car to get in and glanced at the passenger of the deep purple sedan, who was wearing a gold chain around his neck. He smiled and said, "How's it going?" though it was doubtful his voice was heard over the pounding speakers. The thin young man raised his chin in a positive response and then looked away. Ernie then turned to back up the car, and caught a glimpse of the truck driver—a heavy, bearded man also wearing a gold chain. Ernie gestured a wave with his hand as the Beetle began retreating, and the driver acknowledged him with a subtle nod.

"People of different backgrounds are often more alike than they think," Awareness said. "For one thing, everyone wants to have some control in his or her life."

Attidude volunteered his observation. "You know what else they may have in common? I'll bet they both like movies, soda, and popcorn!" And suddenly, Ernie remembered the original reason they were on the road.

Consultant

Oft expectation fails, and most oft there
Where most it promises.
William Shakespeare

Ernie let Willy's phone ring until voicemail intercepted with an invitation to leave a message. "Hey, guy, this is your old man just checking in to see how you're doing. It seems strange we've all gone in separate directions this week, huh? I talked to Mom earlier and she was really excited about her big adventure. I hope you're having a great time too. When you get a chance give me a ring and tell me what's happening. Okay, well, talk to you then. Love you!"

"That went well," Awareness grunted.

"Are you kidding?" Ernie responded. "That's about how the conversation would have gone if he'd answered! Willy just doesn't share much."

Ernie hit the autodial for Karma. Voicemail answered immediately, indicating his daughter was already on the phone. No surprise there. "Hey honey, just your dad checking in. Talked to Mom earlier—sounds like she's having fun—hope you are. Give me a ring and fill me in. Love you!"

"Think she will?" Attidude asked.

"Oh sure, in time. She'll feel obligated."

Ernie's mind drifted into a sea of random thoughts and questions, as if his brain had lost its steering. He noticed that they were again—or perhaps still—in farm country. He noticed a white silo that reminded him of the Tower of Power. He spotted a green tractor, and thought about Obble Legation. Wonder what crops he grows?

"Probably corn. There were more corn fields around Responsibility than anything," Awareness said, answering Ernie's thought.

Ernie realized he was gaining on a slow vehicle. Sure enough, it was the truck patch farmer—again. They passed him unceremoniously for the third time.

"Doesn't he ever run out of gas?" the Dude asked.

"Runs on watermelons," Awareness said dryly.

Ernie thought about Aformation's earlier comment. 'It has never even occurred to him he could fail.' The farmer's simple mission to deliver his melons was almost surely routine, a necessary and familiar part of his process. He would succeed in the effort because he had a clear understanding of all the components—who, what, where, when, why and how. Success was a foregone conclusion because he had clarity.

At almost the moment the word 'clarity' entered Ernie's mind, Awareness pointed to a sign advertising 'The Clarity Bed & Breakfast—*A Destiny City Landmark since 1985*.'

"Too fancy?" he asked Ernie.

"Maybe not. Let's consider it." Ernie realized it was the kind of place Glori would love to stay, and normally he wouldn't consider going without her. But he had thus far spent two fitful nights at inexpensive roadside motels and this *was* his only summer vacation. It was certainly justified...perhaps he would drive by to check it out. Who knows? There were probably no vacancies anyway.

"Why so negative?" the Dude wanted to know. No one answered.

As they rolled on, Ernie's meandering mind landed on the image of the green Beetle parked between the deep purple low-rider and a bright orange high-rider. He was considering their diversity when he caught a glimpse in the mirror of a small car rapidly gaining on him. The little red coupe was in the passing lane but slowed down when it came along side the Beetle, and Ernie looked over to see why. It was a Porsche, and I. Deal was driving it!

Ernie rolled down the window to hear Deal call out, "Ernie, my man! It IS you!"

"Finished with the Newbeckon job?" Ernie shouted back.

I. Deal saw that Ernie was speaking, but couldn't quite make out what he was saying. It sounded like You Reckon Bob, which made no sense. "Let's get off at the next exit!" he suggested loudly and pointed to Ernie, himself, and the road ahead.

Ernie made a thumbs-up sign and watched the movie star businessman throttle ahead and take the lead.   Ernie was thankful the

Porsche then slowed to the Beetle's pace. After settling into a comfortable cruising speed, he added the red coupe to the mental image of the cars at the rest stop, aligned like brightly colored Easter eggs in a parking lot basket.

Ernie followed the Porsche off the next exit ramp, which led to a moderately busy intersection. The two cars turned right and traveled about two blocks when I. Deal whipped the sports car into the parking lot of an empty building. He turned off the engine and was out of the car before Ernie could even get stopped, not a hair out of place. Head held high, he approached the Beetle and waited for Ernie to exit the car.

"I want to show you something," the crane baron stated. "I need your advice."

Ernie climbed out of the air-conditioned car into the midday summer heat. He followed I. Deal around the one-story commercial building with a *For Sale or Lease* sign taped to the window, and then into a cluster of tall trees growing behind it. The two made their way to a clearing beyond and there to Ernie's surprise was an old drive-in theatre, with semi-circular ridges where cars once parked on a slope facing the big screen, which was still standing, though badly in need of paint. Metal poles, once used to tether portable speakers to the cars, were planted throughout the amphitheatre like abandoned tomato stakes.

"Isn't this cool?" I. Deal said excitedly. "And it's for sale!"

"For sale!? Are you thinking what I think you're thinking?" Ernie asked, not sure what to make of the site.

"Maybe. But part of what I'm thinking is that you're just the person to ask." I. Deal began explaining to Ernie that he believed that there was still a great future in the movie business. It had survived the advent of television, video tapes, DVDs, cable services, satellite services, and the internet. "...and yet, people still go to see movies on the big screen, don't they?"

"Yes," replied Ernie. "But..."

"And let's face it, the new generation of teens has only heard about these places from their parents and grandparents. It could be a cool place to gather socially—a kind of retro-cultural experience, like a soda shop or a hamburger stand with car hops. Can't you just imagine kids cruising on Friday and Saturday nights cruising down here to watch the latest horror movie?"

"Well, yes, but..."

Deal continued sharing his idea with the theatre manager. "These days, you wouldn't need the speakers. You could simply broadcast the soundtrack through the car radio. Man, the windows would really steam up if you didn't even need to open them…"

Ernie noticed that I. Deal was beginning to reminisce. It was obvious from his enthusiasm that he remembered drive-in theatres as a magical part of his youth. It seemed to Ernie he may be forgetting as much as he remembered. "I. Deal, do you recall the foggers?"

"The foggers…oh, yeah. Those citronella coils to keep away the mosquitoes! Sure I do. You could buy them at the concession stand."

"And do you remember how hot it was on a summer night?" Ernie wanted to be diplomatic, but his own childhood memories of visits to the drive-in were of swarming bugs, stray headlights, car exhausts, and babies screaming in nearby cars.

"Well, sure. Unless it was winter, and then I remember trying to stay warm without starting the car. Of course, that's in the day of bench seats. Today all the cars have center consoles."

"I'm trying to decide if my own kids would ever visit this place. The truth is, my daughter Karma would prefer to sit in a climate-controlled environment, and my son Willy would rather play video games in the arcade." Ernie watched I. Deal study the landscape while he was listening. But he *was* listening.

"You, know," he finally said. "I doubt my girls would ever come here, either. I guess there is a reason this old place doesn't show movies anymore. I love old boats, but I can assure you there are good reasons they don't build them out of wood anymore. Ernie, I knew you were the perfect person to ask about this place, and you've made me realize why it's a bad idea."

"Oh, no! I don't want to be the one to discourage you. You've obviously had great success with your endeavors. I'm just the manager of a local theatre—not an entrepreneur."

"You're my consultant, Ernie! Don't sell yourself short…we all have our own skill set, and part of yours is knowing what the movie-going public expects. I'm always on the lookout for investment opportunities, but now I know this isn't one of them. I greatly value your advice."

"But I didn't offer any advice."

"Of course you did. I have lots of ideas that get stuck in my head, but I've learned to listen to what the universe is trying to tell me.

Remember, I used to run a sign shop, while there were signs all around me saying I should get out of that business."

Wow, Ernie had never considered himself a part of the universe. In an instant, he recognized Aha's explanation that we're all made of energy—as is everything—and ideas are, in their own way, energy as well. Of *course* he was part of the universe, just as his advice represented the product of his personal energy. "Okay then," smiled Ernie. "Glad I could help."

"Do you have time for lunch? If you do, I'm buying," volunteered I. Deal. "I have something else I want to ask you."

Affirmation

Just Desserts

> There is no meaning to life except the meaning man
> gives his life by the unfolding of his powers.
> **Erich Fromm**
> *[This applies to men and women.]*

As imaginative as Ernie Goforth was, he never imagined he would be eating his lunch on the deck of a waterfront restaurant—on a Tuesday. Yet here he was, at *The Captain's Table* on the shore of Lake Wannafishalot, overlooking docks shared by runabouts, bass boats, pontoons, and one houseboat. They had traveled some distance from the highway to get there, but I. Deal assured Ernie there was a direct route into Destiny City from the lake. A light breeze skimmed the water and the sound of outboard motors was heard in the distance. A few sea gulls, who had abandoned the migrating flock when they discovered this inland paradise, circled overhead, alert for scraps.

Ernie's Pepsi arrived in an iced beer glass, accompanied by a lemon wedge. I. Deal ordered a Perrier with a twist of lime. He sat back in the wicker chair, toasting Ernie with his bubbly drink—his white Polo shirt somehow still crisp despite the drive. His sun-streaked hair was combed perfectly. His designer sunglasses reflected stray light beams bouncing off the brightwork of bobbing watercraft. "I'm really glad I caught up with you today... I've been thinking a lot about our chat from yesterday and your last question."

Ernie took a sip of cola. "What question was that?"

"You asked me something about my *why*. I understood what you meant, but in hindsight it seems a strange way to phrase the question. Or for that matter, it seems a strange question."

Ernie leaned forward, folding his hands and placing his elbows on the table—something his mother would never have tolerated, even in Ordinary. "I suppose it is an odd way to put it, but... well, I've been on a sort of quest lately, and my own *why* is at the center of that."

I. Deal shifted in his chair. "Interesting. So, I take it this trip to Destiny City is more than just an opportunity to talk to the brass about marketing ideas."

"Well," Ernie began. "I suppose it is, but my genuine purpose in visiting Six Sisters is to see how my ideas might be incorporated into operations, and how I might leverage the results into a better paying job." Ernie had practiced this logic so long it actually seemed reasonable. He was even using terminology that sounded more businesslike.

"And you wanted to know what motivates me. Is that so you can compare notes?"

"Not exactly. I genuinely want to understand where your drive comes from. You seem so enthusiastic about everything, and you said yourself you just really enjoy life."

"Well, I do, but I didn't always. There have been times in my life when I thought I was going slowly crazy—my work was difficult, opportunities seemed scarce, and I was barely making ends meet. It affected my home life in ways I'd be embarrassed to tell you about, but I finally realized if anything was going to change, then *I* had to change."

Ernie was fascinated by I. Deal's candor, and by the fact that he had not always been so, well, exceptional. "So did you change?" Ernie blurted.

"Make you a deal. You tell me why you're on your quest and I'll share my story."

Over a shrimp salad and something the chef called a corn biscuit, Ernie shared a summarized version of his story. Thanks to hours alone with the A-Team, he started with the question of 'what had he accomplished in his life?'—or put another way, 'not yet accomplished?'—and how, when finding no suitable answer, he began looking for his life's mission. So far, he explained, he had discovered he had conviction—to not settle for average and to make a positive impact on the lives of others. But he had not yet determined his passion. There was simply no one thing that he could get really excited about.

Deal was a good listener—perhaps, as Ernie would discover— because his was a familiar story. He made good on his promise to share that story, which centered on a lack of purpose, a lack of direction. Eventually, he explained, he realized his natural tendency to feel empathy for others was a strength, and whatever he did should embrace that strength. He told of his own skill set, which included the ability to translate the concept for a sign into a finished, installed product, but how limited capital and strong competition made it difficult to grow his business.

"And then, after a particularly difficult job where I actually lost money, one of my best customers took me aside and lectured me on my ingratitude. He made me look at what I had—a beautiful wife, two healthy daughters—the third one came later—a significant equity in my business, and a lot of contacts. He then suggested that I could keep what works, dispose of what didn't, and build the business in a new direction. So, and this is simplifying it a bit, I adopted an 'attitude of gratitude,' and began writing down what was most important to me and what I hoped to accomplish."

"Affirmations," Ernie said.

"And goals," I. Deal added, "and eventually a comprehensive plan." But I suppose you could say I found my *why* in my own back yard."

"Figuratively speaking?"

"Not really! When I started writing down what was important to me, I realized I had a real connection to the community. Because of my involvement with the sign shop, I often knew when a new business was going to open, I understood local issues of zoning and town growth, and I met lots of roll-up-your-sleeves individuals. I noticed that the people who were accomplishing things were the same ones who weren't afraid of getting involved. When we hosted a birthday party for my daughter in our back yard, I met some parents who were active in local charities and non-profits and I discovered there were real needs in our own town. Well, wouldn't you know it—the same people who were successful in business or achieving their personal goals were the ones helping to meet those needs."

Ernie felt challenged. He could see where this was going, and felt the old insecurities rising inside him. It wasn't that he was avoiding getting his hands dirty, but rather that he felt as if he was just "getting by" himself. Aformation, listening along with the whole A-Team, felt Ernie's apprehension, and whispered, 'I will not decide in advance that I am bad at something.' Attidude added, 'Stay positive, man. This is good stuff.' Finally, Awereness reminded him, 'This is *I. Deal's why*, remember. He's not suggesting it's yours.'

Once both were finished with their meals, and the wait staff took away their dishes. I. Deal said 'thank you' to each of them and continued his story. "After that party, I decided I wanted to be one of *them*. I wanted to be a mover and shaker... a role model in the community. I realized to do that I had to contribute where and how I could make the most impact. I already had the connections. I had developed my talents and expertise. But the first order of business, if you will, was finding a way to free up time to make more money."

I. Deal's tone shifted slightly, and it was evident to Ernie he was now speaking from the heart. "See, the collision of my personal and professional lives was like a train wreck, and though the customer who advised me to keep what works and get rid of what doesn't was talking about my sign business, I knew I had to apply that philosophy to my whole way of thinking. I started by examining what was working in my life and counting my blessings—adopting an 'attitude of gratitude.' And when I did, good things began to happen."

Ernie's apprehension softened. I. Deal was in no way lecturing—he was genuine. And he just gave Ernie a great example of how a person can benefit from focusing on what's really important, or as the story of young Andrew Carnegie's decision to clear the tracks after a real train wreck had suggested, to *burn the cars*.

Ernie pursued I. Deal's phrase *attitude of gratitude.* "Yesterday, you said you contributed to local causes and charities. Was that a part of your comprehensive plan?"

"You betcha. Look, I'm not saying I don't get a payoff from helping other people. It might even be argued I do it for selfish reasons. If I make it a part of my personal mission to give back to the community, it pays off in both emotional rewards and financial rewards. I can't really explain it—but it's like the more I give, the more I get in return."

"Dessert, gentlemen? Our specialty is Key lime pie." Ernie's memory flashed an image of Glori's Key lime pie at the Lumberknot's dinner party—the night Col. Pickett shared his four elements of success. This is another one of those magic moments, he thought, that needs to be celebrated.

"I don't usually order dessert, but that sounds great," Ernie answered.

"Two slices!" said I. Deal with enthusiasm. The waiter acknowledged the order with two fingers that may as well have signified victory. I. Deal smiled his million dollar smile and leaned forward. "I have a personal confession to make."

Ernie imagined the entire A-Team huddling closer to hear this.

"I play this little game with myself. Whenever I see a sign that I've erected, I interpret it as a monument to my success. The more signs around town—or for that matter, around the country—the more success. This of course could be taken literally, as measured in profit.

But for me, it means that I have helped that many more people, while creating more opportunity for myself and others. Remember, Ernie—helping others and making good money are not mutually exclusive."

For a moment, Ernie considered sharing the little game he played, too, except that he didn't see monuments to success, but rather imaginary advisors. Even to the obviously creative I. Deal, this could sound a little silly. So, the A-Team would remain secret. But Ernie did appreciate I. Deal's candor, and knew that the two had every chance of becoming good friends. They shared, after all, a common desire to have purpose in their lives and a passion for achievement.

The pie was excellent.

Martinis and Truffles

Nothing splendid has ever been achieved except by those who dared believe that something inside was superior to circumstances. **Bruce Barton**

Because the shortcut approach to Destiny City was from the lake and not the highway, no clear markings indicated Ernie's precise location until the sign 'Destiny City CITY LIMITS' suddenly appeared. The two-lane road became a divided boulevard, with stately old homes guarded by equally old shade trees and groomed hedges that stood beyond the sidewalks and occasional wrought iron fences.

Awereness pointed to a directional sign indicating the Historical District. On an impulse Ernie turned to follow the route. A few blocks in, beside a mossy cemetery guarding a quaint clapboard church, was a large white house with black shutters and two-story columns fronting a deep rocking-chair porch—way more elegant than the Tombstone Saloon's. At the street, beside a manicured red-brick walkway, an iron post rising from a bed of flowers cradled a beautifully carved sign that read, The Clarity Inn. The temptation to stop was overwhelming.

Ernie found a shady spot in the church parking lot and followed the sidewalk back to the Inn. The house appeared at least a century old, despite the highway sign he'd seen posting a date of 1985. Three shallow steps welcomed him to the expansive front porch furnished with a variety of antique seating venues. An oversized door mat, as wide as the front door and its pair of ornate sidelights, featured a large compass rose, the kind seafarers use to navigate their course.

Ernie wondered if it symbolized the Clarity Inn as a destination within Destiny City, perhaps suggesting the traveler had arrived according to plan. "Oh man, you like, *have* to do this!" encouraged the Dude.

A tinkly bell rang as Ernie opened the heavy front door, and he felt the rush of air conditioning wash over him as he entered the foyer. Below the inside curve of the beautiful staircase sat a Victorian desk, lit by a cast iron lamp illuminating the guest registry placed as if it were a prop in a Merchant Ivory film. A computer screen beside it, however, betrayed the set. Ernie thought he heard someone walking toward the foyer from somewhere deep inside the gracious home.

"Welcome to the Clarity!" said an enthusiastic young woman with short, jet black hair. She had a pale complexion, was 'full figured,' and was dressed in layers of silky, flowing garments—a Whitman's Sampler of pastel vintage fabrics. "My name is Rosalie. Will you be staying with us tonight?"

"Are there any vacancies?" Ernie asked politely. Awereness whispered that she wouldn't have asked if there weren't.

"We have two guest rooms available until Friday—one with an entrance from the courtyard, and one up these stairs. Both have private baths. Are there two of you?"

Ernie smiled to himself, suddenly having the image of the entire A-Team with him. "No, just me. I'm in town on business for a couple of days."

"May I make a suggestion then?" Rosalie asked.

"Yes, please."

"Both rooms are beautiful and well appointed, but the one upstairs is maybe a little goopy for a guy. I mean, it has this lacy canopy over the bed and a pink bathroom…"

Ernie held up his hand. "I understand, you're right. Maybe the courtyard room would be better. Rosalie then went over the prices and schedules. There would be Afternoon Tea—which was really a wine social—each day from 4:00 to 5:00. Breakfast began at 8:30. He was a few minutes early for the 3:00 p.m. check-in, but that was okay, and check-out was by 11 a.m. She processed his credit card and explained where to park. As she leaned over the desk drawer to find his room key, Ernie noticed a tattoo on the back of her neck, the tip of a larger image that disappeared beneath her gauzy layers. She then stood up and asked him to follow her.

Rosalie swished as she walked, her airy sleeves and shawl flowing like Actionman's cape. She wore elaborate earrings with a tiny skull among the beads, and smelled like lilacs. Ernie could easily picture her as being one of the six sisters in his antebellum fantasy, perhaps representing 'Miss Where.' She led him through a short hallway off the foyer and through what Ernie surmised was once a servant's entrance into a private brick courtyard, completely fenced off from the street except for a high, solid gate. Holding out the key ring for his inspection, she explained, "This one is for the gate, this one is for the house, and this one is for your room." Ernie saw her gesture and turned to see his room door, flanked on either side by elaborate ironwork painted green and featuring oak leaves, over which a small plaque read, THE ACORN. Rosalie noticed him smile as he read it, and said, "Sort of a silly name, I guess. The other rooms are named after trees—Magnolia, Dogwood... I think the owners thought this room with its separate entrance was like a little offshoot of the Inn. You know, like a little acorn that fell off to the side of the big tree."

"It's the perfect name," Ernie said.

Rosalie stood near The Acorn's door as Ernie explored his temporary domain. It was enchanting—cool and quiet and accessed through a shady courtyard; light years more elegant than the fleabags he'd been staying at along the highway. "Let me know if you need anything. Otherwise, I'll see you at Afternoon Tea?"

"Probably—yes—thank you." Ernie watched the young tattooed woman sashay through the courtyard and disappear into the main house. He left through the courtyard gate to move his car and gather his things. All the while, Attidude was jumping up and down like a kid who's just been offered ice cream.

"I've been meaning to ask you," Ernie said to the Dude. "Whatever happened to your megaphone?"

"Oh, man, I dropped it back there at Chances R, where the fat guy almost ate you. Anyway, you don't need me as much as you used to. I haven't had to shout for days."

As Ernie moved the Beetle from the church parking lot, he realized Attidude was right. In just a few days, his outlook on life in general had improved, and he sensed his future was perhaps a little brighter. He had finally arrived in Destiny City, where the magic was supposed to happen. He'd stumbled into—actually, he'd followed the signs—to a great mission base camp appropriately named The Acorn. And tomorrow he would meet with Morris Better.

Back in The Acorn, Ernie looked at his cell phone to make sure there were no messages from Karma or Willy, and was surprised to discover there was indeed a text message. View Now? Yes. The message was cryptic: cmp s gr8 tlk l8r w.

"What does 18r mean?" Ernie asked Awereness.

"I think that's L8R, as in LATER," the wolf man speculated.

"I am grateful Willy answered his phone, and even more grateful he's having a good time," affirmed Ernie, practicing I. Deal's attitude of gratitude.

"That one should be in our book, soldier," Aformation said. Ernie retrieved the yellow notebook from his bag and looked at his watch. Still 45 minutes before the Afternoon Tea. There was time to write notes on his Tombstone Saloon epiphany, the subject of gratitude, thoughts on keeping what works and discarding what doesn't, and the concept that to receive more you have to give more.

"Is that what I. Deal said exactly?" Awereness questioned. "I don't think it's a bargaining kind of thing. You don't give in order to receive or it wouldn't be giving at all."

Ernie realized he needed to record these new insights carefully or their meaning might be lost. He also remembered his need to rephrase the earlier principles to reflect what he *does,* rather than what he *will do*. He buried himself in the notebook, and the remainder of those 45 minutes passed quickly.

At 4:02, Ernie studied his disheveled appearance in the mirror, and decided to invest in a quick shower before joining the Clarity gathering. By the time he arrived inside, the antique grandfather clock struck 4:15 and three couples were enjoying wine and hors d'oeuvres. Rosalie was swishing from guest to guest, happily pouring the wine and occasionally testing it herself. When she saw Ernie, she introduced him to the others as Mr. Goforth.

"Call me Ernie," he said, shaking hands with a short, dapper, middle-aged man sporting a handlebar mustache.

"And you call me Angelo," the diminutive guest offered. "What brings you to Destiny City?"

"I was going to ask you the same question," Ernie said. "Actually I'm here on business. And you?"

Angelo, whose full name Ernie later learned was Michael Angelo Martini, was—along with his wife Olive—on a trip across the country to visit family. "We've not seen our nephew since he was in high school," explained Angelo. "And now he has a family of his own." Ernie, fresh from reviewing and updating his yellow notebook, recognized immediately the Martinis had a specific what and a specific why. He also realized their purpose represented the Family in F.O.R.D.

Olive joined them, eager to meet Angelo's new friend. Ernie introduced himself and deliberately chose another F.O.R.D. topic. "So what do you do for fun, Olive?"

Mrs. Martini, with dancing, dark eyes and naturally beautiful skin, flipped her salt and pepper hair flirtatiously before answering. "I draw and paint," she said, obviously pleased to reveal her passion.

"She's a great artist," Angelo said proudly. "I can't draw a straight line, and she can capture the soul of a flower."

Ernie smiled at both his success in striking a chord and Angelo's appreciation for his wife's talent. "So she's the artist and you have the artist's name," he teased.

"Yes!" said Angelo. "It's why she married me!" They talked briefly about her achievements, her gallery exhibits, and her dreams for the future. Angelo gave Ernie her card and invited him to visit her website. After thanking him, Ernie excused himself to sample the wine.

At the serving table, another guest was eyeing a chocolate truffle, debating whether she should embrace indulgence. The trim woman appeared bookish, wearing conservative eyeglasses and a lightweight brown sweater. Ernie could sense her reluctance, and encouraged her. "Think of it as weight control—these are really appetite suppressants. You won't eat as much at dinner."

"I like your reasoning," she said, smiling but not looking directly at him. "By that logic, perhaps I should take two."

"Well, after all, it is part of the Clarity experience. May as well enjoy all it has to offer." By now, Ernie was anticipating her decision, betting she would succumb to her desire. When she did—select *one*, that is—she finally looked directly at Ernie and said, "Shame on me," and then smiled.

"I'm Ernie Goforth," he said in hopes of getting her name.

"I'm Eleanor Crump. Do you always lead people into temptation?"

"You know, I've never thought of it that way, but I suppose I do." Ernie used his facial expressions to communicate surprise. "I run a movie theatre and a big part of that business is concessions," he explained. "And I believe the cinematic experience should include pleasures of the palette."

"I don't go to many movies," Eleanor said. "I suppose if I did I would be fat."

They continued their conversation by the grand piano, where Angelo joined them. The three briefly discussed the merits of film, and how these days, presentation seemed to outweigh content. "Of course, storytelling tools have been sharpened by technology," Ernie submitted. "*Safety Be Damned—in 3D* is a pretty impressive film." As the topic drifted from movies to literature, Ernie asked if either of them was a writer. It was a way of establishing the Occupation topic of the F.O.R.D. theory. But Ernie also genuinely wanted to know.

Angelo deferred the question to Eleanor. "No, I'm a middle school teacher," she answered. For the next several minutes, Ernie was able to relate to her vocation thanks to having two kids who were—or had been—in middle school. Somewhere in the conversation about "finding one's self" Ernie realized some important things about Willy's evolving maturity—and about the personal payoff he was receiving simply by offering his attention to this thoughtful, unassuming woman. When the dialog paused, he reflected on her generous insights as well as those of I. Deal—'It's like the more I give, the more I get in return.'

Ernie looked at his watch and realized Afternoon Tea would soon be over. "Is that your husband talking to Rosalie?" He nodded in the direction of a bald man in khaki shorts and tennis shoes.

"Yes, that would be him. And you're right—he's the one talking. Poor Rosalie—I hope she likes sports."

"Rosalie is a good sport herself," Ernie reflected aloud. "She really brings this old place to life."

"Yes, she's a good fit, considering the Clarity's history."

"What do you mean?"

"You know, about it once being a funeral home. And about its reputation for being haunted."

"Actually, no, I didn't know that," Ernie readily confessed. "Is that in the guidebooks or something?"

"Oh, heavens no. Bad for business. But most people around town have heard the stories. Have you noticed that Rosalie dresses as if she were a ghost?"

Ernie looked over at the hostess and her swaths of chiffon. He caught a glimpse of her earrings, reminding him of the tiny skull he had noticed woven into them.

"She does look sort of 'ethereal,' doesn't she?" Ernie was doubtful the Clarity was connected to the spirit world, but acknowledged Rosalie may be convinced of it. "You say this used to be a funeral home?"

"For sixty-one years. We're standing in what was one of the viewing rooms."

Ernie looked around at the heavy crown molding and the beautiful chandelier. He could imagine the foyer serving as a reception area, with velvet ropes leading twentieth century residents to their dearly departed in various main-level salons, and offices and conference rooms upstairs. Just outside the window he could see the cemetery and the church—it all made sense. He remembered his first impressions and thinking this place could be a final destination within Destiny City. How right he was!

The Afternoon Tea was breaking up—Rosalie was saying goodbye to Mr. Crump and the Martinis had already left. Ernie decided he would meet the others at breakfast.

"Well, I enjoyed talking with both of you," Eleanor said.

"It's been a pleasure," Angelo replied.

"For me too," added Ernie. He then turned to ask Eleanor one last thing. "I'm curious—how did you know about The Clarity's history?"

"Oh, I'm a bit of a history buff. Our first visit was in the late eighties and I did some research then. In fact, they were still working on some parts of the house—adding the courtyard in the back and the outside door to the embalming room."

"Wait—that guest room off the courtyard was where the funeral home embalmed their, uh, clients?"

"Yes. That's where they got them ready to 'plant.' In fact, now they call it *The Acorn*. Well, I guess I'll see you at breakfast. Good night, Ernie."

Wine and Spirits

We suffer primarily not from our vices or our weaknesses, but from our illusions. We are haunted, not by reality, but by those images we have put in their place.   **Daniel J. Boorstin**

"It's freakin' me out, man! Freakin' me out..." Attidude had climbed to a new positive plateau only to lose his footing. Awereness noted The Acorn room had no indication it had ever been a clearing house for the dead. "Yeah, that helps a lot!" the Dude said sarcastically.

"What difference does it make?" Awereness asked. "Even if it's true, the bodies brought here were already deceased—nothing evil took place."

Actionman began looking in all the corners and under the bed. "That's *silly*," the wolf man scolded. "If there was ever any sign of death, it's been gone for more than two decades."

Attidude began to calm down. Awereness was right. The school teacher's history lesson had nothing to do with today's reality. The Acorn was just a room in an inn, regardless of what might have transpired a generation ago. Nonetheless, Ernie felt agitated and restless.

Why hadn't Karma called?

Ernie decided he'd waited for his daughter to return his call long enough. He dialed her number, and again the phone went straight to her voicemail. Something was wrong. He dialed Glorianne's number, then hung up before it rang because he didn't want to say anything to alarm her. He decided to try again later. He knew her friend's parents had all the other parents' numbers in case of an emergency...

The wine on Ernie's empty stomach was compromising his composure, and sitting on the bed, he felt drained of energy. Perhaps he was a little embalmed himself. He kicked off his shoes, lay back on the welcoming mattress, and felt the cloud softness of the Clarity's feather pillows. His mind drifted. Unlike the Goodnight Inn or the Owl's Nest, there were no road noises—no noisy room air conditioner. No tump... tump... no...

Ernie awoke to the obnoxious ringtone of his cell...*Tell me somethin' good!* He glanced at his watch—8:30!? A.m. or p.m.? A quick glance at the window revealed only a dim light and he still wasn't sure. He did not recognize the number, but the area code was the same as his own. "Hello?"

"Dad?"

"Karma! What's going on? I left a message, uh, this morning but..."

"So you *did* call. I'm so sorry. My phone got dumped in the ocean and I didn't know you called. Mom told me you were going to call, and... Dad, I'm sorry."

"It's okay, honey. I'm just glad the phone drowned and not you. What happened?"

"Oh, we were horsing around on the edge of the surf and someone threw a Frisbee and... well, it's a dumb story. But I think it's ruined. It won't turn on."

"Other than the phone, is everything all right? Are you having a good time?"

"Oh, yeah!" Karma sounded as excited about the beach trip as her mom had about Cosmic Encounters. She had been to a water park, played miniature golf, had a cookout on the beach, tried calamari for the first time, buried a boy in the sand up to his neck...

"Buried a boy? Where did *he* come from?" Ernie wanted to know.

"It's okay, Dad. We dug him up before the tide came in."

"Why? I'd have left him for the crabs. Where did this boy come from?"

"Oh, he and his friends were playing volleyball in front of the beach house and we got to know them, that's all. It's totally cool."

"Where were Whitney's parents?"

"Oh, Dad. I'll tell you all about it when I see you. It's all good."

"Well, I'm glad of that. Promise me you'll stay out of trouble, okay."

"Okay, Dad. Well, I'm on Whitney's minutes so I better go. Sorry about my phone."

"Don't sweat it. We'll get you another one. Be careful, okay?"

"Bye, Dad—love you."

"I love you too, Honey."

Well, it had taken all day, but at least he made contact. The kids were safe, and apparently happy. Attidude's agitation had subsided and the nap had cured much of Awereness' irritability. But Actionman was hungry. It seemed like he was *always* hungry.

"Let's go get something to eat!" the caped figure begged.

"Okay, let's do." Ernie granted. Since his quest began, it seemed like every interesting conversation, every revelation, every discovered principle was realized in the presence of food.

Ernie locked The Acorn behind him before exiting his private courtyard gate. The sun was low in the sky. It would undoubtedly be dark when he returned. The Beetle was now parked in a gravel parking area across a narrow street, perhaps appearing on the map as an alley, behind the Inn.   It was the first time he had seen the back of the old funeral home from any distance, and it seemed considerably larger than the Victorian-era houses around it.

Ernie realized he had not seen anything of Destiny City beyond the historic district he accidently discovered when driving from Lake Wannafishalot. He had been to the City twice before—once for the hiring interview nine years earlier and once for a corporate pow-wow when Six Sisters merged with another company three years later. Both times he had arrived by plane and had limited time to see anything but the section of town where headquarters was located. This was new territory for him.

He drove back to the boulevard that led him to The Clarity and pointed the Beetle toward town in the hopes of finding a commercial district—or at the very least, a passable restaurant. In a matter of blocks he saw a familiar sight—the characteristic Six Sisters logo above a multiplex marquee featuring the headline movie, *Safety Be Damned—In 3D*. He could almost smell the popcorn. But with only a light lunch and two glasses of red wine consumed in the past eight hours, he needed something of substance to keep Actionman from complaining.

A few more blocks revealed two choices—an Italian eatery and a Japanese steak house. 'In honor of my new friends the Martinis,' he concluded as he parked the car beside an elaborate fountain hosting a trio of bathing Roman gods. Ernie entered the Leaning Tower of Pasta through a series of stone arches and torches with simulated flames. It was a much fancier place than anything Ordinary had to offer, and despite the hour, they were still serving!

Once inside, Ernie heard a waiter singing in Italian. A lady costumed in black sequins welcomed him and introduced him to Vincent who would gladly seat him. 'Fancy shmancy!' as his father used to say about free mints at the local cafeteria. Once seated, Ernie munched on parmesan breadsticks while he explored the menu map of Italy.

"I'll have the mussels and linguini," he told the waiter wearing black pants and a white apron. "But just water tonight, thank you."

Ernie's waiter—a short fellow named Tony—apparently was not of the singing variety, but he certainly looked Italian. When he asked Ernie if it was his first visit to the Leaning Tower, one answer led to another and Tony discovered Ernie was staying at The Clarity. "A friend of mine works there," he said. "Have you met Rosalie?"

"Of course. I get the impression she runs the place."

"She practically does—at least, through the week. There's a night manager and a different one on the weekends. Did she give you a tour of the house?"

"No, I've only seen the main floor and the courtyard. I'm staying in the The Acorn."

"Oh... the room off the courtyard." There was a brief pause. "So you haven't seen the attic."

"No. What's in the attic?"

"Oh, there's just a really cool room up there. You know the Inn used to be a funeral home..."

"Yes, I've heard that."

"Well, I better put your order in! I didn't mean to talk your ear off!"

"That's okay, Tony—we'll talk more later."

"You wanted to stay someplace other than a roadside motel, right?" Awereness reminded him.

"What do you think is in the attic?" Ernie asked the wolf man.

"What or *who?* We'll ask Tony."

Ernie ate the last breadstick and sat quietly at the candlelit table. The live singing had been replaced by recordings of Frank Sinatra and Dean Martin. He imagined the Disney movie *Lady and the Tramp* and the two pups sharing a common strand of spaghetti. He imagined Willy at camp eating "a big pizza pie," Karma at the beach with a basket of popcorn shrimp, Gloria in the jungle cosmically encountering a vegetarian power meal—if there was such a thing. He thought about I. Deal sitting on his dock eating barbecue, Mrs. Broaderbuht substituting popcorn for dinner, and Obble Legation eating every leftover from the Chances R kitchen.

Ernie allowed his imagination to keep the cinematic images rolling. Four popcorns at the Acorn Festival, thirty syrups at The Pancake Palace, Key lime pie at The Captain's Table, chocolate truffles at the Clarity Inn... Good grief! More than finding different ways to enhance his career, this trip had been about finding different ways to *eat!*

"It's one thing *everybody* has in common," Awereness concluded. Ernie resolved that at tomorrow's meeting with Morris Better, he would place a special emphasis on the part of his presentation involving snack options.

Ernie sat up straight and previewed the entree as Tony placed it in front of him. "So what's in the attic?"

"The attic? Oh, you mean at The Clarity. Just a room where they conduct, uh...parties."

"Parties?" Ernie quizzed. What kind of parties would they 'conduct?' he wondered. Then he remembered Eleanor's claim that the place was haunted. "You mean they hold séances?"

Tony poured more olive oil for non-existent breadsticks. He smiled uncomfortably and shrugged his shoulders. "Sometimes Rosalie likes to act like she's communicating with spirits, but it's just for fun. It's an excuse to have a party, really."

"Really." Ernie used the term more as punctuation than to question. How interesting. Tony weaseled out of the conversation with a grandiose wrist gesture, accompanied by the request to "Enjoy!" Throughout the meal, he refilled the water twice, but no more was said of Rosalie or her spirit world.

The pasta was delicious. The mussels, a rare treat. The last time Ernie had shellfish was at the Lumberknots—another example of food being a thing everyone had in common. Ernie declined dessert and left a generous tip.

The moon was almost full on the first night of his trip, and now on the drive back to the Inn it appeared completely spherical, though it was hard to be sure because drifting clouds partially obscured it. Ernie entered the private gate and locked it behind him. Crickets serenaded the antique neighborhood. The wolf man seemed restless.

Ernie stood silently, enjoying the warm summer night air and the light breeze propelling the clouds. Perhaps it was the nap, or the recently ingested calories, but he wasn't quite ready for bed. He sat down on a park-like bench and looked up again to examine the moon but found a different light source instead, somewhat dimmer. It was coming from a small window above the second floor—the Clarity's attic.

Actionman was watching, too. "Let's go check it out."

"No, let's don't," replied Ernie. "Let's sit here and enjoy the moment." A car passed slowly through the narrow street on the other side of the tall fence, out of sight except for the headlights' scattered reflections. Ernie pictured the old Cadillac Cathedral Hearse he'd seen parade down Main Street in White Oaks. That very machine could well have served this funeral home.

Ernie thought of the people buried in the cemetery next door and how many of them may have passed through this place, by way of the room reserved for his evening's sleep. He wondered what they had accomplished in their lives…what legacy they had left for the generations that followed. Perhaps his room once served as a sort of way station between life and legacy.

The light in the attic was still on. Why was it that every attempt made at some form of cosmic communication took place from the highest point possible? Aha's clients realized their personal energy from the Tower of Power. Churches' steeples reached toward heaven. I. Deal even created a way to erect towering monuments to motivate his continued success—"spires to inspire."

And yet, Ernie was still on the ground floor. He decided his assigned room would be his own way station, a stop between his old life and his new one. It was, after all, named The Acorn, and as Stephen Longfellow had explained to middle school graduates, the acorn holds the blueprint for an entire oak tree—a huge result from a tiny seed.

"That's great!" Attidude said. "We can embalm the old Ernie and resurrect a new one."

"Thanks a lot," mumbled Ernie, not caring too much for that particular image.

"We better prepare for tomorrow, don't you think, soldier?" asked Aformation. Suddenly Ernie felt tired at the very thought of going over his notes for the meeting. And then, the courtyard became brighter. Looking up, Ernie saw the entire full moon for the first time, and in the corner of his eye, he saw the attic window go dark.

Action

Balconies and Basements

> Up, sluggard, and waste not life. In the grave
> will be sleeping enough. **Benjamin Franklin**

Allof the guests staying at The Clarity Inn had gathered in the dining room by 8:36 a.m. In fact, Ernie was one of the last to arrive. There were the Martinis, the Crumps, the other couple Ernie never got to talk to at Afternoon Tea, and one couple he did not recognize. Rosalie, who worked the day shift, amazingly greeted everyone by name and reintroduced them all. The breakfast plan, she instructed, was to begin at the buffet for fruit, juice, and coffee or tea, and the staff would ultimately serve main dishes once everyone was seated. Ernie found himself in line behind an older woman named Dorothy who, clueless, prevented an orderly traffic flow by painstakingly preparing her hot tea at the buffet. While he waited on her patiently, Ernie noted Rosalie's Wednesday wardrobe—similar to Tuesday's except this time in shades of charcoal and black.

Angelo was spirited and began talking with others while his artist wife Olive struggled to smile. She nursed her coffee, grasping the cup with both hands as if it were a religious artifact. Eleanor used one hand to gather her sweater and the other to sort the fruit on her plate. Her boorish husband assumed Ernie was interested in the DC Decimators, a team Ernie surmised played baseball. He tried his best to stay focused but found himself listening to three conversations at once, at one point hearing Dorothy asking someone if the church next door held Wednesday night services. Eleanor was quiet but chose a moment when her husband finished a familiar story to wedge in a question. "So how did you sleep?"

Ernie knew what she was really asking—what was it like sleeping in a converted morgue?

"Very, very quietly," he teased. "Actually, having a moonlit courtyard just outside the door and a private entrance made for a pleasant environment."

Eleanor smiled like Mona Lisa and stirred her coffee. Rosalie, still swishing, helped a young woman in a white apron distribute egg casserole, bacon strips and sausages, and an assortment of sweet rolls and flat breads. The conversations stalled only briefly. "Which room were you folks in?" Ernie continued.

"We're in The Loblolly—one of the ones with a balcony," the sports fan replied.

Ernie raised his eyebrows. "I didn't realize any of the rooms had balconies," he confessed.

Eleanor explained, "The two at the end of the hall share a balcony, on the other side of the house from the cemetery. I like to sit out among the tree limbs and read my book." The servers had arrived at Eleanor's setting and she arched her back to allow room for Rosalie's reach, her arm swathed in a cascading sleeve.

"I'll be back with some more coffee for you in a minute, Mrs. Crump," she said. "Oh, and I found that book on Destiny City Architecture you were asking me about. I'll bring it too."

"Thank you, Rosalie."

The tinkling sound of silverware tapping dishes and ice cubes jostling in glasses provided audible proof that guests were enjoying their breakfast, even as the conversations continued. Olive was now awake enough to comment on the local arts scene, and Dorothy's white-haired husband talked about an amazing gospel singing group he had heard on Sunday. Ernie watched Rosalie return with the coffee pot in one hand and a gray, hardbound book in the other. When she stopped by Eleanor, she set the pot down long enough to search out a specific page in the book. "Here it is," she said, and handed her the open volume. Eleanor adjusted her glasses.

"Ernie, you might be interested in this," she said as she handed him the book across the table. Ernie was careful to keep it open to the same page, and studied a sepia-toned photo of the very structure he was sitting in. It seemed even more imposing in the old picture—a minimum of shrubbery and only a few young trees caused it to appear almost sterile. A low, horizontal sign in the front yard, now long gone, read Polter & Gyest Mortuary. Two men in dark suits stood stiffly beside it, their faces offering no discernable expression.

"Wow, what a great old photograph!" Ernie said as he studied it. By now Rosalie had brought the coffee pot to his side of the table. As she was refilling Ernie's cup, he pointed to the photo and asked her, "What are these eyebrow windows on the roof? Is there a third floor?"

"Oh, those are in the attic," Rosalie said matter-of-factly. "It's just a storage area. There are no real guest rooms up there."

Ernie hesitated for a moment, then ventured, "Funny, I thought I saw a light on up there last night. Is that possible?"

"Yeah, I was up there last night after work. My boss, the owner, lives out of town and when he comes here to visit he sometimes sleeps up there. He's coming this weekend so I was fixing up his little sleeping area—fresh linens, clean towels—fluffing it up for the master of the house."

Ernie considered leaving the explanation alone, but couldn't resist taking it another step. "I'll bet it's a great place to escape from the constant stream of guests. You could have a party up there and no one would know!"

"And we've had one up there—the boss doesn't care. Last Halloween we had a pretend séance, this bein' an old funeral home made it especially creepy, and we had a lot of fun. Mostly it's just a place to store old files and some extra furniture."

Ernie felt like a detective without a case. There was a simple explanation for the light in the attic, and once again his imagination had invented an illusion. Rosalie was so innocently forthcoming he found it hard to believe she embraced any kind of sorcery. As she emptied the remaining coffee into Mr. Crump's cup, Ernie asked one more question, trying to sound nonchalant. "If this was an old funeral home, where did they prepare the bodies?"

"Down in the basement, I've heard. Where The Acorn is now there used to be a back room with a set of stairs accessing the basement, but they took all that out when it was made into an inn. Now the only way to get to the basement is through some narrow steps coming down from the pantry, and all that's down there is the furnace and a bunch of spider webs.

"Man, she's no fun at all." Ernie heard the Dude whisper. So much for summoned spirits and haunted hallways. From what Rosalie said, Ernie's room was actually the newest part of the house and had nothing whatsoever to do with death. He didn't know whether to be relieved or disappointed. Eleanor made a facial expression that said, 'Who knew?'

"Don't you think that's how conspiracy theories get started?" Awareness whispered. Ernie thought of the snarling man back at the garage in Pruneville, and glimpsed an understanding of how misunderstandings, rumors, and irrational fears can foster suspicion.

Breakfast concluded with a decadent crumb cake, or as Eleanor's husband joked, a Crump cake. Slow Dorothy and the gospel music enthusiast left first, followed by the couple Ernie never did meet. When Mr. Crump began to wind down from his story about athletes and false-positive drug tests, Ernie decided to bail. "It was nice chatting with you both," he said, deliberately making eye contact with Eleanor last. "Enjoy the balcony," he added.

Back in the Acorn, Ernie opened his packet of proposal outlines and looked over them one more time. His appointment with Better was at 10:30, so there wasn't much time to rehearse, but at least he remembered the presentation sequence. He added the necktie to his wardrobe and slid into his suit coat. His reflection in the mirror didn't look so much like good ol' Ernie as it did Mr. Goforth. Behind his mirror image emerged Aformation.

"Remember your commitment to mastery, son. *I master my personal energy by embracing excellence, ignoring negativity, and rejecting limitations. I recognize that average is not acceptable, and use the commonplace as a foundation to build uncommon results.*"

Ernie had booked the room for two nights. He would not leave Destiny City before tomorrow. But the big day—the day that would potentially change his future—was today. From the modest Acorn, a mighty career would grow. As he turned from the mirror, the image of Aformation disappeared. Ernie grabbed the presentations and headed for the Beetle.

Better and Worse

The manager asks how and when;
the leader asks what and why.   **Warren G. Bennis**

Finding the Six Sisters corporate headquarters was not difficult once Ernie found the highway. His travel notes were accurate, and though the neighborhood had changed in the five or six years since his last visit, there were enough remaining landmarks beyond the highway exit to guide him without turning around once. He was in the parking lot at 10:20.

Ernie entered the lobby, feeling transformed into Mr. Goforth, a man on a mission. He gave the receptionist his business card. "Oh, hello Ernie. I'm Evelyn. We've talked several times on the phone."

"Nice to meet you in person, Evelyn. How's everything in the front office?"

"I'm just glad to be working!" She said immodestly. People are having a time these days, aren't they?" Ernie noticed she didn't say anything about the office. The interior and furnishings were exactly as he remembered it.

"I have an appointment with Morris Better. Could you tell him I'm here?"

"I'd be happy to, but I don't think he's in yet," she said apologetically. "But let me make sure." Evelyn dialed his office and Ernie could hear a phone ringing faintly in the distance. No one answered. "Just a minute." She held the receiver at an angle and pushed a button. "Morris Better-uh. Morris Better-uh. Please call the operatore-uh." Evelyn's intercom voice echoed throughout the building. "Just have a seat, Ernie. I'm sure Mr. Better will be here shortly."

Ernie had a seat just across the room from Evelyn, but not so close as to seem a pest. She was as steady as they came. Ashe Lumberknot would call her a good soldier. He sat quietly until 10:40 and then took out a copy of his presentation to read once more. Half way through the second page, he overheard Evelyn talking quietly on the phone to someone. "Would you tell him Ernie Goforth is here? I think Morris had an appointment with him at 10:30. Yes. Okay, thaaaank you." After the call, Evelyn continued typing some shipping labels.

Around 10:50, Ernie excused himself to use the men's room. As he walked quietly down the carpeted hallway, he could see Morris' office. A glass wall separated it from the larger room filled with cubicles, and noticed that the lights were off. Ernie checked out Mr. Goforth in the mirror—he still had an air of confidence about him.

Ernie's watch read 11:07 when Evelyn received a call that had to be Mo Better. "I'll tell him," she said to the caller before hanging up. "Ernie, that was Mr. Better. He said to tell you he had been delayed at a vendor's place of business but is now on his way, and to say he's sorry to keep you waiting."

"That's fine," Ernie responded pleasantly, suspecting it was a hollow excuse. At least he was on his way.

Better finally arrived at 11:40—an awkward time, Ernie thought, for a presentation that he'd hoped to complete comfortably before lunch, in case some of the others needed to leave. What Ernie did not realize was that there were no others. "Sorry, guy!" Better said as he extended his hand. "Things are just so hectic these days, and there's just not enough time to juggle everything. How was your trip? Did you fly in?"

Ernie knew perfectly well that he had told Better he was taking the week to prepare and drive the distance expressly for this meeting, but did not want to start the conversation on a negative note. "Nope," he said, "I decided to drive." From Better's distant look, he wasn't sure the V.P. had heard the answer, but he *was* sure he didn't care. Better seemed distracted, if not disinterested. Maybe I. Deal was right about him.

"Let's go in here," he said, and signaled Ernie to follow. They went into a small, bare conference room with no furniture but a round table and four battered chairs. The setting reminded him of the little conference room at the Ordinary Observer. At one time along his trip, Ernie felt he had not prepared well enough. Now it seemed as if he had spent way too much time organizing his thoughts on paper.

"First of all, Morris, I appreciate you taking the time to see me. As I mentioned in my email, I have some ideas I think the entire management team might be interested to hear." Suddenly Morris got up and shut the door. Ernie was sure the gesture was not meant to counter what he'd just said, but it seemed that way. He continued.

"I've written out some ideas based on a year's worth of observations in my theatre—opportunities I believe can lead us to enjoy a positive impact on our company's bottom line." Better sat with his elbow on the table and his chin in his hand. He was looking at Ernie but did not seem to be engaged. The table was small enough that at one point he simply reached over and grabbed the packet to retrieve a copy of Ernie's outline for himself.

"This first page I think would be of particular interest to our accountants," Ernie continued. "It shows how fully two thirds of concessions are sold before..." He stopped talking when he realized Better was not looking at the stats, but instead was flipping through the pages.

"This is good stuff, Ernie. I'm eager to show it to some of the management team. Can you leave me a copy?"

"Well, of course, but it's only an outline. Don't you think it would be better for me to explain what it references to the various department heads?"

"Well, a lot of the guys are on vacation. Anyway, we've got some new programs worked out with our vendors and I'm not sure we'll be approaching concessions in the same way after the summer."

"I understand, and I'm actually happy to hear that. If you'll look at page 3, you'll see that I have some suggestions..."

"Shoot, man! I plan to look at it all. But you know what? I have a lunch date today and maybe we can find some time to sit down once I've read over it. How does that sound?"

Ernie was furious, but did his best to conceal his anger. "Do you think we can try this again after your lunch appointment?"

"You mean this afternoon? Uh—I'm not sure. Let me check my schedule and..."

This time it was Ernie who interrupted. "Morris, let me ask you something. If I showed you how you could triple your concession profits throughout the system by this time next year, would you have any interest?"

"I expect I would. Is that what's in here?" Better snapped the stapled papers in the air.

"No. What's in there are my efforts to identify opportunities for enhanced sales, not specific formulas or timetables or profit projections. But if I promise to come back with a comprehensive plan, will you promise to assemble the entire management team to hear it?"

Better frowned at this aggressive tone. He could see Ernie's face was red, despite his measured words. Maybe it would benefit him to listen. Morris Better could be the hero who increased company profits if the plan worked, and Ernie Goforth could be the scapegoat who squandered resources if it didn't.

"When do you want to meet again?" Better asked, calling Ernie's bluff.

"How about tomorrow morning at 10?"

"I'll have everyone here. I'll even have Tory here. Thanks for coming in, Ernie—we'll see you tomorrow!"

Tory! Ernie felt a twinge in his gut. Victor Tory was the CEO of the theatre chain. His reputation for extravagance and dynamism was legendary—and his temperament was rumored to be unpredictable. Ernie could as easily be dismissed from the company as promoted—no one was above Tory on the corporate ladder. Ernie struggled to contain his fear.

"You can do this, man." Attitude seemed supremely confident. "You will impress the big guy." Ernie hoped this was true and felt a never before known sense of pride that he would have a chance to speak directly to a legend.

Mo Better, however, was everything I. Deal had said he was—and worse. Ernie stopped at the front desk to speak to Evelyn while Better continued out the door, mumbling to the receptionist he would be back in an hour or so. She looked at Ernie with sad eyes and sighed. "You know he's the son of one of the original six sisters, which means he's the nephew of the other five."

"Explains things," Ernie said grimly, deciding that those two words were almost too many. "Evelyn, do you think you could fix me up with an empty office and a phone?"

"I think we can arrange that," she said supportively. "One of our department heads is on vacation," she added, and then whispered, "and another one who is gone I doubt is coming back."

In a matter of minutes, Ernie was sitting at an empty desk in a remote corner of the building with not only a phone, but a computer. He used the internet to look up addresses and phone numbers, cross referencing his memory with maps of all the places he'd been on his journey to Destiny City. He had an idea—one that came so suddenly and with such clarity he thought it had to have been there all along, as if it came from somewhere else in the universe. His mind swarmed with the different concepts he had collected along his meandering path to this moment—the acorn's blueprint for a mighty oak, the channeling of personal energy, the 'foregone conclusion" of success.

Ernie began to connect the dots of his experience and skills. There was a shift in his attitude, he became aware of a great opportunity, and he was confident his idea would work. He just needed a detailed plan of action, but the first step was obvious: he had to let go of old ideas so new ones could emerge.

For the next five hours, Ernie worked steadily until Evelyn knocked on the door and told him they needed to lock up. Only once did he take a break, and while in the men's room washing his hands, he thought he saw in the mirror a billowing cape around his own shoulders. If Morris Better ever returned from lunch, he was not aware of it.

On the way home, Ernie looked at the homework he had stacked on the passenger seat. His packet of presentations had grown into a file box of folders full of notes, printouts, and hand-scribbled flow charts. It was evening rush hour and he had missed Afternoon Tea altogether. Breakfast was finally wearing off…and he needed to get out of this suit.

He turned into the narrow road behind The Clarity and this time drove beyond the graveled parking area to see if he could glimpse Eleanor's balcony on the Inn's far side. Sure enough, there it was, carved into the roofline like a wide dormer missing its walls. But Eleanor was nowhere to be seen. He wondered if her comment about reading books on the balcony was fiction, as imagined as her story of the Inn being haunted. Or, on that subject, perhaps she had jumped to the conclusion about the Inn too early, without a clear understanding of the facts. After all, Ernie had also made assumptions that proved to be inaccurate—about his mission, about Morris Better, and about himself.

There all along

Success is 10% inspiration, 90% last-minute changes.
From a billboard advertisement

Ernie showered, brushed his teeth, and sorted through his remaining clothes until he found a shirt similar to the one I. Deal had worn at The Captain's Table. Dressed for a casual dinner, he left The Acorn but rather than head for the car, entered the main house and navigated his way to the front desk. There sat the night manager, a woman who was *not* Rosalie.

"Hi, I'm Ernie."

"Hello, Ernie. The Acorn, right? I'm Shirley Wood."

Ernie liked Shirley immediately. She was the opposite of Rosalie in appearance—trim, tan, and tailored. Rosalie's short hair was jet black. Shirley's long hair was so blonde it almost glowed. "How did you pull the night shift?" Ernie wanted to know, assuming the evening schedule was a less desirable time slot.

"It was my choice," she said confidently. "Are you enjoying your stay here?"

"Yes, very much, especially once I realized the ghosts weren't interested in me."

"Oh, that old rumor. It just won't...die." She smiled knowingly. "Who told you the place is haunted?"

"I guess I convinced myself, after misinterpreting different comments." Ernie told her about Eleanor Crump's mistaken belief that his room was once used for embalming, how the waiter at the Leaning Tower spoke of séances, how even Rosalie had the appearance of an apparition when she floated through the room in her wispy wardrobe. "And then, last night under a full moon, I saw a light on in the attic..."

Shirley was laughing out loud. "The attic? Are you sure? Oh, that's right! Rosalie was up there last night getting the room ready for Daddy!"

"Daddy?" Rosalie's comments about 'the boss' flashed in his mind. "Your father is the owner?"

"Yep. Job security. Actually, this is, or will be, my house. It's supposed to be a family business, but Daddy doesn't have time to look after the day-to-day affairs, and Mama refuses to leave the condo in Boca Raton. So I look after things.

Ernie didn't remember Rosalie ever using the boss's name, but he assumed it was also Wood... unless that was Shirley's married name. "Is that the reason all the rooms are named after trees? Because your name is Wood?"

"You guessed it!" And the room you're staying in was named after me. It was the room I played in as a child, that is, after Daddy removed some stairs to the basement."

"But your name is not... oh, I get it. You're the little acorn that came from the tree—the little Wood."

"You're pretty good at making connections," she said. Shirley went on to say she had majored in marketing and recently received her MBA, specializing in product development. "Rosalie said you're here on business?"

"Yes. Today I worked through lunch at Six Sisters Cinemas. As a matter of fact, I was planning to go get something to eat, and was hoping you might recommend a little tavern or something. But you just said something that intrigues me...You said your specialty was product development?"

"Yep."

"Wow... I could sure use your help on a project I'm working on. Normally I would bounce ideas off my wife but she's..." Ernie realized he was beginning to ramble, and decided to stop explaining and simply ask. "Could I hire you as a consultant just for tonight?"

"I'm not that kind of girl."

"Oh, no! I'm talking strictly business here." Ernie could feel his face turning red. "See, I have a big presentation in the morning and I need someone to help me refine a couple of key points. I think you may be the perfect person to provide some analytical feedback—that is, if you don't have anything pressing planned."

"What if we ordered some pizza? I can eat my 'savory chicken and rice' microwave meal some other time."

"Pizza it is! Thank you, Shirley. You showed up at exactly the right moment."

"Actually I've been right here all along. You're the one who just showed up."

Over the next few hours, Ernie shared his insights and plans with the young businesswoman, answering her questions and listening to her critiques. Pizza and Pepsi fueled the session and by the time they fine-tuned the program and agreed little more could be done without actual vendor agreements, it was time to call it a night. This was the meeting he had hoped to have with Six Sister executives earlier that day, but scheming with Shirley was infinitely more productive, and undoubtedly more fun.

When Ernie offered to compensate her for her assistance, she exchanged her fee for a promise that he would always stay at The Clarity Inn when visiting Destiny City. It was a promise he would keep.

That night, Ernie drifted into one of his cinematic dreams, this one taking place in The Clarity dining room. Breakfast was about to be served, and all the characters of his journey were there—Obble LeGation sat beside his tiny mother; blue eye-shadowed Pert sat beside her shy daughter Charlie. Routine was talking to Sir Syrup while the juggler floated twirling breadsticks overhead. The scowling man from the Slick & Quick garage sat beside Oprah Winfrey. Rosalie, wearing a large white apron, brought a tray of corn dogs and chocolate truffles from the kitchen. Two Heathers scurried about refilling cups and glasses. Ernie wondered if, given the setting, they weren't all ghosts.

In the dream, Ernie left the dining room for the Inn's front porch, where he encountered the Who/What/Where/When/Why & How sisters all gathered around Scarlett O'Hara. An invisible orchestra played "Tara's Theme" and once again Ernie heard the voice of Gerald O'Hara, except this time he realized it was Aha doing the talking. "You mean to tell me, Katie Scarlett O'Hara, that flavor doesn't mean anything to you? *Food* is the only thing that matters. It's the only thing that everyone desires." And then Scarlett turned and looked directly at Ernie to say, 'tomorrow is another day.'

.

Two Years Later

Guest of honor

> The difference between involvement and commitment
> is like ham and eggs. The chicken is involved; the pig
> is committed.   **Martina Navratilova**

"**A**nd in the "Most Creative New Packaging" category, first place goes to Stephen Longfellow, for *Obble-Gobble Party Popcorn!*"

Stephen Longfellow took the stage at the regional Addy Award competition amid hardy applause. It was no surprise to anyone when the innovative popcorn package took top honors. As Ernie had assured him, success was "a foregone conclusion." Stephen had learned from Ernie that it took more than inspiration to succeed in a creative mission. It took the four A's.

The other packages in the advertising association competition, though colorful and nicely printed, were fairly routine designs. Nobody else had die-cut arms and legs attached to a popcorn bag that, when heated in the microwave, expanded into an enormous fat man. Thus, Obble-Gobble was the competition's only 'brand to expand' in a comically literal sense. Kids loved watching the thin man grow fatter and fatter. Parents liked watching their kids enjoy a snack healthier than most.

Ernie was among a small fan club of personal supporters in the audience to give Stephen a standing ovation, because through his innovative design, Steven had helped expand the upstart flavored popcorn division from a product available only at Six Sisters Cinemas to a national sensation. He was a late addition to the team of talented participants in the new Six Sister's subsidiary Obble-Gobble Unlimited—among them product developers, commercial kitchens, printers, warehouse distributors, bookkeepers, and salespeople, all reporting to Ernie. But perhaps the most important member of the team was the source of the product, Obble himself, who provided the raw popcorn from his family farm in Responsibility. His image not only graced the package design—it *was* the package design.

By the time Stephen's consumer package was adopted, Obble-Gobble Party Popcorn was already well-known to anyone visiting a Six Sisters Cinema.   There was even evidence to suggest if a movie was playing at competing theatres, moviegoers would choose Six Sisters just to try a different popcorn flavor. And what flavors! Most adults preferred nostalgic notions like *Caramel Apple* and *Parmesan Storm* while kids loved the wacky ones like *Grass Clippings* and the best seller, *Beehive Swarm*. (This one was Karma's invention—discovered one night when she added too much cinnamon to the honey coating recipe.) Record popcorn sales had prompted Six Sisters' management to restructure their entire concessions strategy around the Obble-Gobble product line within a year of its introduction.

After the last award was presented and the regional ad club president thanked all who participated, Ernie invited Stephen and Robert to join him by the pool at his 'new' old home in the Ordinary's historic district. Glorianne and the kids would be there, and they had something to show them. Steven was flattered by the gesture, and agreed to drop by. Ernie said, "See you there!" and left the Civic Center parking lot in his little green Porsche.

Along the shady street in front of the Goforths' place—a recently remodeled Victorian home—several familiar cars were parked. Ernie waited for his guest of honor to arrive before closing the garage door, and the men walked through a side courtyard to arrive by the pool. There on the wrought iron and glass table were all 24 Obble-Gobbles—24 paper men already popped full—in 24 different flavors. Each one had been propped up from the back to appear as if he was sitting at attention, and Karma—with the help of her friends—had salvaged old doll clothes and miniature fashion accessories to "dress" each one. Willie had used his computer to create a banner serving as the table's apron that read, *Congratulations to a Longfellow—from 24 short fellows*. Stephen expressed surprise and gratitude. Robert, forgetting yet again to act like the accomplished attorney he was, jumped up and down, applauding the popcorn panorama. "I just *love* it!"

French doors on the house opened and several guests spilled out. The senior Obble-Gobble Unlimited consultant, Ashe Lumber-knot, extended his hand to Stephen and expressed his genuine appreciation. "Everywhere I go, people are talking about their favorite flavor," Lumberknot reported. Cherry Lumberknot, whose role in the company was to oversee the distribution of charitable funds, told Stephen that his clever ideas had an indirect but substantial impact on the community.

"Who'd have thought a little paper man could generate such interest?" she asked rhetorically.

Stephen replied, "It's not the package. It's the content. And for that, we have only Ernie to credit. He's the one who had the brainstorm...the one who realized he could marry fun and profit."

Ernie said, "Well, actually, all I did was connect the dots. The demand, the know-how—even the different flavors—were already there. I just matched up the right combination of resources. But I really think the business isn't even close to reaching its full potential, because one thing leads to another. You want to tell them about the latest, Stephen?"

Everyone on the patio was listening: Mrs. Broaderbuht—who now ran the multiplex in Ordinary, Vince and Trula Pickett, two of the Iron Butterflies who now worked in the Obble-Gobble warehouse, the Goforth children Karma and Willy, who had been a part of the enterprise from the beginning, and four other OGU 'teammates.' Stephen smiled and said, "We're working on a new ad campaign that will have the Obble-Gobble man dancing on TV. And Willy is doing the computer animation!"

Chants of "Wow!" and "Super!" rose from the crowd as their gaze turned to Willy, who in the last two years had experienced a growth spurt of his own and was now taller than his dad. Ernie watched Willy's response to the adults' genuine appreciation of his extraordinary talent, and knew this moment would have a profound impact on his maturing attitude. In fact, Ernie thought, he looks a little like that old imaginary friend Attitude—a little disheveled, unruly long hair, and a not-quite-sure sense of self.

"Someone's here to see you," announced Glorianne from the patio door. Ernie looked up to see a short bald man dressed in a simple white tunic and sandals.

"Aha, our spiritual leader!" Ernie had long figured out the popular advisor was no monk, but that his image had been cultivated for people who understand that spirituality is a key component to success. Aha did not pretend to be an ordained anything, but rather a counselor for folks whose conscience objected to religious hierarchy. Aha never used guilt, shame, or fear as tools to extract moral behavior or money—his approach was less judgmental and more respectful. He simply helped people recognize their personal potential—for a fee, of course.

"Hello, Ernie! Hello, Trula—Butterfly Ladies—everyone!" The familiar sing-song speech pattern was now comforting to Ernie—it was, after all, Aha who had helped bring Ernie and Ob LeGation together. Aha was introduced first to Mrs. LeGation, who had once seen him interviewed on television. The kind 'monk' was able to persuade her to consider Ernie's proposal as a way to brighten her loyal son's future, something he would never have suggested if it weren't true. She didn't realize her oversized offspring would also become famous in the process. Now the local TV station wanted to interview Obble!

"My goodness!" Aha exclaimed as he examined the fat little popcorn men dressed in Hawaiian leis, cowboy hats, and vests that wouldn't close. "They certainly are full of themselves!" He then turned to the guest of honor and asked him how he got such a great idea. Stephen confessed he wasn't sure—it just "came to him" in the shower. Aha closed his eyes, smiled, and nodded.

Ernie couldn't be happier. All around him were family and friends gathered for a festive occasion and most of them were also now his business associates. He loved his job; he had made a positive impact on almost everyone he knew—even if in a small way. Thanks to Victor Tory's sponsorship, his business returned a respectable profit, as well as a comfortable income. Perhaps the most welcome side effect was the impact on his family, all of whom had caught Ernie's infectious enthusiasm—his new passion to channel his energy and make a difference in the world.

Glori's was perhaps the most dramatic change. Shortly after returning from the Costa Rica workshop, she applied her Cosmic Encounters education to real life, with satisfying results. She had realized so much of her personal life had been invested in her children, partly because their dad was often absent, that she had suppressed her own ambitions. Now that they were older and pursuing their own interests, she felt less needed. While Ernie was searching for his *why*, she was too, except she hadn't framed it that way. At the workshop, she felt alive again, making close friends and trying new things. And back at home in Ordinary, she wanted to feel that same energy. When a teacher for whom she'd substituted called one evening to ask her if she would consider tutoring a student, she said 'yes' almost without thinking. After the success of her one-on-one experience with the boy who would have otherwise failed English, she knew her talents as both teacher and mom had a rewarding purpose.

Now, two years later she was in demand as a respected and sought after tutor, and she loved it. Ernie, though busy as ever, was able to work around her schedule if a parenting demand required it, and appreciated the support of his happier, more confident wife. And though her popcorn flavoring ideas had merit, her best work in the kitchen was baking pies.

"Who wants some Key lime pie?" Glorianne asked as she brought out two pies on a tray. Little time was wasted slicing and distributing the creamy, cool treat.

"This is outrageously delicious!" her excitable fan Robert said. "Can I have the recipe?"

"Sure—I'll even share what I *add* to the recipe," she said, hinting there were hidden ingredients to success. "But no one must know but us," she warned with a wink.

Karma, standing just within earshot, repositioned herself to whisper into Robert's ear. "All she adds is a little flavoring from Obble-Gobble *Tropic Thunder*, and it was my idea." Robert raised his forefinger to his lips to indicate they were sealed. Tropic Thunder was a surprise to most popcorn lovers, employing an unorthodox mixture of mint and lime to echo the taste of Ashe Lumberknot's favorite drink, the Mojito.

"Where do you guys come up with these ideas?" he asked Karma. She explained that they do a fair share of experimenting at taste parties, which her dad insists on calling saloon sessions. When they think they're onto something, they enlist the help of a woman over in White Oaks named Pert Near. She and her daughter Charlie then refine the formula for a recipe that can be scaled up for large batches. "Amazing!" he said. Robert had handled legal contracts between OGU and it's distributors but had little knowledge of product development.

Ernie tapped on an empty glass with a spoon to get everyone's attention. "I'd like to propose a toast," he announced. "To our energetic and brilliant Stephen, who has helped our team more than he knows."

Everyone raised their glasses in the air, "To Stephen!"

Ernie then reached in his pocket, adding "I have a little package for you," and produced an acorn. A few people laughed, not in on the symbolism. But it wasn't lost on Stephen, and he accepted the acknowledgement with a facial expression that could only be interpreted as heartfelt appreciation.

The group mingled for awhile and took turns congratulating the guest of honor, eventually offering their good wishes and goodbyes. Ernie finally got around to eating the last piece of Key lime pie, and his mind drifted to his first visit to Lake Wannafishalot and the dessert shared with his close friend, I. Deal. 'We have a lot in common,' he thought, and scanned a mental inventory of overcoming obstacles, finding creative solutions, and helping others. They were both in control of their destinies; they were both passionate about their purpose. Ever since the first road trip to Destiny City, they stayed in contact. And when Ernie told him of plans to create a new company, I. Deal was the first in line to offer his help—not for personal gain, but to really help—which started with a phone call to Vic Tory. Last summer, the Deals even invited the Goforth family to visit them on the lake, and when they accepted, Ernie made reservations at The Clarity. It was there that Karma met Shirley Wood, who persuaded the upcoming high school junior to consider a career in business. All this, he reasoned, because he was able to find his *why*. He felt deeply an attitude of gratitude.

Fond Farewell

Henceforth I ask not good-fortune,
I myself am good-fortune.   **Walt Whitman**

When everyone had left and the pie was just a memory, Ernie studied the Obble-Gobbles sitting in formation on the table. Each one had the same goofy smile. Each one had the same steam vent slightly open at the neckline, as if the big man's overalls strained to stay fastened. For just a moment, Ernie considered giving each flavor a personality, the way he had once done with the four A's of Col. Pickett's success formula. But that seemed silly, not because of the fantasy factor, but because it was, well, unnecessary. All four members of the A-Team were part of each little fat man already, just like the journey that inspired their creation. They were the results of Attitude, Awareness, Affirmation, and Action, and those 'personalities' were already packaged in each popcorn person. Ernie reflected on Aha's lesson that everything (from the T-shirt to the TV) began as a thought, and that thought itself was energy. Party Popcorn packaged energy in more ways than one.

Ernie turned his head to identify a shadowy figure he noticed in the corner of his eye. It was a werewolf.

"Awereness! I haven't seen you in what?—a year or more?"

"Been here all along, man. You just don't need me as much as you used to. You're pretty practiced at staying alert these days."

"I suppose it's become a habit." With those words, Aformation appeared, standing erect with his ever-present clipboard.

"Practice *becomes* habit," he said. Ernie had not seen the old soldier lately, either.

"I still read my affirmations every once in awhile," Ernie said. "But these days I'm living them without having to remind myself, or rather, to depend on you to remind me."

Attidude peeked around the corner and continued Ernie's thought. "We know how important it is to *embrace excellence, ignore negativity, and reject limitations*. It's called *mastering our personal energy*. Attidude looked more polished than Ernie had ever seen him.

He sat staring at his old friends, and realized one was missing. "Where's Actionman?" he asked.

Awereness glanced at the others before answering in his characteristic coarse whisper. "Are you kidding? Man, these days *you* are Actionman."

The A-Team slowly faded away into the recesses of Ernie's busy mind. They had accomplished their mission of helping transform a muddling wanderer into a purposeful achiever. The following day, Ernie accidently found the tattered yellow notebook in the Porsche's glove box and carried it inside to his home office, a room accessed by the courtyard behind his Victorian home. He placed it on a shelf among some treasured keepsakes that included the program to an Ordinary Middle School graduation ceremony, a torn road map, and a menu from the Pruneville Pancake Palace.

Interview

Say "Yes" to the seedlings and a giant forest cleaves
the sky. Say "Yes" to the universe and the planets
become your neighbors. Say "Yes" to dreams of love
and freedom. It is the password to utopia.
Brooks Atkinson, *Once Around the Sun*, 1951

"Hi, Mr. Goforth? I'm Al Wright from the Ordinary Observer.
We spoke on the phone?"

"Yes, Al. I've been expecting you. Come in."

"Mr. Goforth…"

"Call me Ernie."

"Okay—Ernie, I must admit when our editor asked me to
interview you, I was excited. Your popcorn is a favorite at our house,
and I think the Obble-Gobble company is the biggest thing to happen
to Ordinary in a long time."

"Actually, it's Obble-Gobble Unlimited, and it's a division of
Six Sisters Cinemas, Inc. But it's nice to hear your family likes our
product."

"Everybody likes your product. It's really made a big impact
on the movie industry, and for that matter, the popcorn industry!" The
reporter was slipping into hyperbole.

"No," Ernie stopped him, smiling but shaking his head. "That's
how rumors get started… It's true we've been well received, but there
are always challenges with any start-up, and we have some obstacles to
overcome. To say we've made a big impact on the movie industry is a
huge overstatement."

"Okay, I've already admitted I'm a big fan. So let me get the
facts straight." For the next 30 minutes Ernie answered Wright's
questions—mostly about his inspiration, how the product was
developed, and plans for the future. Ernie wanted to answer the
questions accurately, but he also wanted Wright to know the answers to
a few questions not asked—how it was an important part of the
business plan to participate in community events, to provide funds to
causes like literacy programs and free clinics, and when possible, to
hire the disabled. Ernie assured him it was in the company's best
selfish interest to 'give back.' If, for example, he provided popcorn for
a worthy cause, the organizers were grateful for the assistance and
Obble-Gobble found new customers.

"Are you saying that your motives for charitable giving are self-serving?" Wright challenged.

"Of course they are—but in a good way. Helping people and making money are not mutually exclusive. People afraid of letting go of 'stuff' often become hoarders. People who can't accept change usually become bitter. And people afraid they will lose happiness if they share it don't understand how the universe works." Ernie realized he was beginning to sound like Aha, which surprised him.

"Would you call that your philosophy of success?" Wright asked, pad in hand.

"If you want a philosophical quote about success, here are my suggestions—*Be aware of the opportunities around you. Connect the dots. Listen to the universe. Believe in yourself.* And possibly my favorite: *Lead with a passionate plan and success will follow."*

"Excellent. Well, thanks for your time—and insights, Ernie."

"May I ask *you* a question?" Ernie asked.

"Of course."

"What ever happened to the wife and child of that policeman who was electrocuted a couple of years ago? Did he leave any kind of legacy?"

Wright stared at Ernie, his facial expression changing with recognition. "Wait a minute—I remember now! You're the same guy who came to my office that day asking why the man died—and I asked you who can know why anything happens. Right?"

Ernie smiled and nodded. "So, did you ever figure that one out or is it still unknowable?"

"Well, I know the community was very supportive of his family and a lot of people felt his death was a great loss. You know, maybe it's as simple as his death reminded a lot of people how precious life is—how important it is to make the most of it and contribute to society. Is that what you get from it?"

Ernie answered, "Yes." For an instant, suspended in time and space, his mind engulfed the word. It was just three letters—representing an affirming answer. Of course, there was still no way of knowing for sure why the policeman's life ended, but Ernie was no longer afraid to accept a simple answer. It was a very different response from the days when Aha accused him of having an "Oh, no!" moment—at a time when *No* was the easy answer to everything from embracing a party game to investing in himself.

Glori had said *Yes* to tutoring, and it made a huge difference in her life, which in turn made a positive impact on Ernie's life. If universal energy has polarity, *Yes* registers positive. When someone sees the opportunity to make a difference, to make an impact—even to help out in some small way, the best way to answer the call is to say *Yes.* Would he go to Destiny City? *Yes.* And would he be open to change? Would he find his passion? *Yes,* he thought. *Yes.* He would do this because to succeed, you have to try. And to agree to try, you have to say *Yes.*

And because, *Yes* begins with *Why.*

An Alternate Choice

> I think you have an obligation to be an optimist.
> Because if you're not, nothing will change.
> **Ron Silver**

"No, today we're walking this way," the young woman explained to her three-year-old. The little girl was justifiably confused. When she walked to the park with her mother, they usually turned right at the end of their driveway. "Let's see what it looks like on this side," she encouraged.

Of course, the pretty single parent already knew what it looked like. She just had not mustered the courage to revisit that intersection over the last two years. Only four blocks from her house, it was the corner where her life had changed forever one midnight, followed by the morning her handsome young husband never came home. It was the intersection that was featured on the 6:00 news the following evening, reporting to all of Constant County that she was now a widow.

"I want to go to the swings, Mommy," the little voice pleaded.

"We will, honey—but we're going a different way this morning." It was time, she had decided, to take the last step of putting it all behind her—an act of catharsis she would avoid no longer. She and her young companion would pause briefly to look at a new power pole where the broken one had stood, to study the area where a car suddenly went out of control, to imagine the darkness and confusion her husband had experienced when first arriving on the scene. He had only been on the force for eighteen months. For others, the terrible accident had become a sidebar in the journal of life's mysteries; for her, it was still the front page.

"When we get to the park, you can swing and slide and play in the sand," the young woman told her daughter. "And then we'll have a picnic!" Having a snack at the park had become a sort of tradition. They had always carried some water and some snacks on their walks.

"Obba-Gobba, Mommy? Obba-Gobba?"

"Yes," she assured. "I brought popcorn." Obble-Gobble was now the treat of choice—a healthy indulgence. She considered its occasional use as an appropriate incentive—or even in some cases a bribe—for inducing good behavior. It was a pardonable sin, a means to justify an end. Before flavored popcorn, the child's favorite snack was Cheerios. In fact, she used to take them with her on walks in her stroller.

Oh, No! or Aha?

The young mother would never know that there was a correlation between the innocence of her child and the death of her husband, and it might be argued that they are no more related than any other random events. But even tiny shifts in the universe can have a profound effect on our lives. All things are interrelated in ways we cannot begin to recognize or fully understand. To quote an old song lyric, "little things mean a lot."

The young mother would also never know that her child's innocent behavior would indirectly influence the creation of a new enterprise and positively impact the lives of so many people. The ripple effect of the smallest actions, which begin with ideas, intentions, or even random thoughts can be profound. Though it's impossible to know precisely *how* our thoughts and actions will influence our future, it's certain that they will.

Thus, just as seemingly insignificant events can cumulatively effect a negative outcome, the same can happen to create a positive result. We may not have control over our environment, but we can exercise control over our attitudes. We can correct—rather than protect—irresponsible actions. We can choose to be positive rather than negative.

There will always be spills, from a few Cheerios, to a trainload of diesel fuel, to millions of gallons of crude oil. There will always be obstacles to clear, fears to conquer, and bad habits to overcome. We can blame them for our underachievement or we can find new ways to adapt and prosper. It is not an overstatement to say those who dwell on negative thoughts doom themselves to an unhappy life.

In the end, our positive energy has the most potential to create positive results. In some cases, we may even choose to create a new life for ourselves. But before we can know *how* to begin that journey, we must know *why*.

Ernie's Recommended Reading List

Stories of Uncle Adrian – Zan Monroe
As A Man Thinketh – James Allen
Secrets of Question Based Selling – Thomas A Freese
Think and Grow Rich – Napoleon Hill
The Go Giver – Bob Burg and John David Mann
Go-Givers Sell More – Bob Burg and John David Mann
Linchpin – Seth Godin
Why We Make Mistakes - Joseph Hallinan
Selling the Invisible – Harry Beckwith
What Clients Love – Harry Beckwith
Mr. Scmooze – Richard Abraham
Unlimited Power – Tony Robbins
Customer Satisfaction Is Worthless – *Customer Loyalty Is Priceless*
    – Jeffrey Gitomer
Endless Referrals – Bob Burg
Blink – Malcolm Gladwell
Outliers – Malcolm Gladwell
Permission Marketing – Seth Godin
The Magic of Thinking Big – David J Schwartz, PhD
Mastery – George Leonard
The Power of Focus – Jack Canfield, Mark Victor Hanson, Les Hewitt
Never Eat Alone – Keith Ferrazzi
The Master Key System – Charles Haanel
How to Win Friends and Influence People – Dale Carnegie
How to Stop Worrying and Start Living – Dale Carnegie
The Traveler's Gift – Andy Andrews
Hug Your Customers – Jack Mitchell
The On Purpose Person – Kevin McCarthy
The On-Purpose Business – Kevin McCarthy
The Answer – John Assaraf
The Success Principles – Jack Canfield
The Happiness Hypothesis – Jonathan Heidt
Three Feet From Gold – Greg Reid And Sharon Lechter
Vital Friends – Tom Rath
First Things First – Stephen R Covey
The Little Engine That Could – Watty Piper